WORKAROUNDS

How to Conquer Anything That Stands in Your Way at Work

THAT WORK

RUSSELL BISHOP

Editor and columnist, *Huffington Post*

New York   Chicago   San Francisco   Lisbon   London   Madrid   Mexico City
Milan   New Delhi   San Juan   Seoul   Singapore   Sydney   Toronto

The *McGraw·Hill* Companies

1 2 3 4 5 6 7 8 9 10 11 12 13 14 15 16   DOC/DOC   1 9 8 7 6 5 4 3 2 1 0

ISBN   978-0-07-175203-9
MHID   0-07-175203-X

Library of Congress Cataloging-in-Publication Data

Bishop, Russell, 1950–
        Workarounds that work : how to conquer anything that stands in your way at work / by Russell Bishop.
            p.   cm.
        ISBN: 978-0-07-175203-9 (alk. paper)
            1. Organizational effectiveness.   2. Performance.   3. Problem solving.   4. Workflow.   5. Management.   I. Title.

        HD58.9.B497   2011
        650.1—dc22   201029959

McGraw-Hill books are available at special quantity discounts to use as premiums and sales promotions or for use in corporate training programs. To contact a representative, please e-mail us at bulksales@mcgraw-hill.com.

This book is printed on acid-free paper.

For Valerie, my loving wife, friend, and constant reminder
that God must love me

Contents

Foreword

first met Russell Bishop in 1978 when I participated in a self-development seminar he was leading. Within the first hour of the event I told myself, "I'm going to work with this guy!" He was demonstrating a mature command of core principles of effective behavior along with an uncanny knack for making them real, digestible, and immediately usable for an amazing range of people and circumstances. This was true "life" education, in my view, and gave me a star to follow in my own career.

I fulfilled my prophecy, spending several years in close quarters with Russell professionally and personally. Our collaboration planted and nurtured the seeds of what was to become the core of my work in productivity—the Getting Things Done (GTD) methodology. My respect for him as a mentor in working with the dynamics of human interactions hasn't wavered over the decades. I'm thrilled that he's made much of his understanding and cogent advice available in these pages.

This book tackles a neglected arena in the professional development environment: the people and behaviors that have to work well together in the vast gap between the world of "leadership" and the real-world requirements for day-to-day execution. Too often the landscape is littered with business gurus, off-site retreats, and organizational-change consultants that run counter to corporate training programs focused on practical skill building and core business processes.

Executives wind up staring at their navels, challenged to think about what their company wants to be when it grows up.

Worker bees stare at their computers, taking online courses on how to work their customer databases and other systems. People at both levels—top and bottom—can easily feel like victims of circumstances.

The executives, managers, supervisors, and key sole contributors at the heart of organizational performance frequently become squeezed between lofty initiatives generated at the C-levels and the plethora of projects and people that drive real-world growth and success.

This is messy territory, populated by smart, high-performing people who find themselves caught in the inevitable conflicts that arise between vision and the structures that emerge to institutionalize it. These folks have the responsibility to grapple with multiple ambiguities, figure out how to deal with them, and produce results, no matter what. I've spent much of my time and research deep down in the trenches with these folks, one-on-one, attempting to get a grip on what the "work" really is and what needs to happen to accomplish it. Invariably some of the most imperative matters to deal with involve elements that they feel are out of their control. They've been dealt a hand, and they are expected to win the pot, come what may.

Most all of us want to go somewhere and have some idea about how to get there; however, our practices and procedures frequently seem to get in the way. Those experiences are as often the result of our own internal making as of the external restrictions we rail against. This challenge is equally shared by the chairman of the board and the new hire on the front line, each of whom struggles with conflicting commitments, diverse constituencies, and immediate demands on time and responsibilities. The solutions, likewise, will be shared by all of us.

You won't read anything in the following pages that you don't somehow already know, and know that you should do—nor anything that you don't immediately have the resources to address. Of course, that's likely true of 99 percent of the suggestions in the huge library of business self-help books, not to mention the abundance of diet, exercise, and create-personal-wealth how-to manuals. The difference here may be the elegance of the understanding of the issues along with formulations of the tricks we can employ to address them. This is subtle and sophisticated stuff, but Russell has made it accessible as a game that we can all play—and win.

It's in situations of challenges and constraints that we seem to optimally grow. Creating workarounds that work may be a key part of our existence here.

—David Allen, author of *Getting Things Done*

Acknowledgments

A long the way toward getting this book, many stand out as friends, supporters, colleagues, and guides, each contributing to my growth and development. David Allen, Ben Cannon, John O'Neil, Sally McGhee, Jeff Bowden, and Jack Canfield each encouraged me to take bigger risks, to expand in the face of contraction, and to rise to new levels of service.

Many have encouraged me to write, none more than Arianna Huffington, to whom I owe a great debt of gratitude for her decades of support and the opportunity to hone my skills writing for the *Huffington Post*.

Thousands of clients, graduates of seminars I have led, and colleagues along the way have contributed to my learning the nuances and differences between good ideas that *should* work and the practical solutions that *actually do* work. I would like to thank the global Insight community for the opportunity to serve over the years and to Candace Semigran and Dr. Greg Stebbins in particular for keeping the vision alive.

Anton Gueth, Mark Gordon, Lynn Darnton, Heide Banks, and Deb Robbins have each offered encouragement and the occasional kick in the seat of the pants to keep this moving forward. Of course, without the foresight and support from Gary Krebs of McGraw-Hill, this book would still be languishing in the back of my brain somewhere. My agent, Doe Coover, took on all kinds of details and helped me stay focused.

Without the marvelous contributions of those who sat through interviews with me, none of this would have come to life. Tony

Schwartz, Dave Logan, Michael Winston, Marshall Goldsmith, David Rosener, W. Mitchell, Irwin Carasso, Tim Dayonot, Armondo Martos, Dr. Andrew Heaton, Sally Bishop, Sean Finn, Tray Cockerell, and Evan Taubenfeld all contributed significantly to the development of these ideas.

Finally, my deepest love and appreciation go to my spiritual mentors and loving spurs in the side, J-R and John Morton—thank you for keeping me mindful of who I really am in midst of all this. And, of course, to my loving wife, Valerie, for her constant trust, love, and commitment to the highest good for all of us.

Introduction

I n the day-to-day world of business, all manner of situations show up that require workarounds. Sometimes workarounds are fairly innocuous, and other times they can be pretty risky. My principal concern in writing this book is that many people turn to workarounds when they perceive someone else as the problem. My experience suggests that indeed, sometimes the other guy can be a pain, but then, so can I! Therefore, I want to steer clear of the blame game and look more closely at what I can do—what *you* can do—that will make a difference without having to engage in blaming someone else first.

One major key that will be emphasized throughout the book is the notion that the first workaround may actually start with you! It's not that you are the problem or someone to blame; still, it could be that something about your own thinking or mental approach to the challenge needs to shift before anything meaningful can take place elsewhere. In fact, you will see that in this book, I am championing letting go of blame and complaints altogether in favor of taking even more responsibility for the solution you need.

In just about any situation, the first question to ask is: "What could I do that would make a difference that requires no one's permission other than my own?" As you will see, this simple but powerful question may be all that is required to move from road-block to effective, productive action. To be sure, you may well need to enlist others in the process, but the first workaround may be merely the mental shift that says, "I can do something about this on my own." Maybe you won't be able to get everything done on your own, but starting with your own approach to the problem may help get things unstuck.

A workaround could be as aggravatingly mundane as being at the airport, learning that your flight has been canceled, and having to come up with alternative plans. Or it could be considerably more complex, involving your boss, senior leadership, other teams, or even your customer. And it could be a combination of simple and complex, such as trying to work through something with another office worker who isn't quite as helpful as you might like.

SO, WHAT IS A WORKAROUND?

You have probably encountered the term *workaround* before. For our purposes, we will define it as a method for accomplishing a task or goal when the normal process or method isn't producing the desired results. Workarounds can range from the simple to the complex, from the temporary to the permanent. In the information technology world, a workaround is often described as a temporary fix to overcome hardware, programming, or communication problems. Once a problem is fixed, the workaround is usually abandoned when subsequent releases come out addressing the bug that created the problem in the first place.

THE WORLD'S FIRST COMPUTER BUG

The term *bug* as applied to electronics first came into common usage when a Harvard Mark II computer ran into some operating problems back in 1947. The engineers trying to identify the source of the problem eventually found a moth that had flown into a relay and prevented it from working.

They taped the moth into the logbook and labeled it as the first bug ever having been found under such circumstances. While the term *bug* had been used for some time to describe unknown issues, going as far back as Edison, the discovery of an actual "bug" led to the term's being used to describe anything that prevents a system from operating normally.

Workarounds can also be quite imaginative, reflecting even more out-of-the-box thinking than the original piece of software or hardware. However, software workarounds are rarely permanent solutions and do not respond well to increasing pressure or increasing frequency of use. Clearly, there are a fair number of unintentional bugs gumming up the works in our businesses these days. Some of the workarounds that this book will suggest have the potential of working over the longer term, but as with the software world, under pressure, even the best workarounds will need attention lest they become their own kind of bug!

How and Why to Apply Workarounds to Your Job

It may seem as though something slightly more significant than a moth has flown into one or more relays at your company, preventing an important task from being done or blocking a whole project from completion. If you want to get the project moving again, you may have to do some creative thinking to come up with a workaround that will work, without causing even more damage to the system.

Bugs or roadblocks come in all kinds of flavors:

- A key player is out of town, and you can't move forward until he or she returns.

- Another team is late with its part of the project.

- Something is stuck in the communication or approval process.

- A process once considered important or efficient is either out of date or missing key parts.

- Teams that should be working together have conflicting priorities.

There are many more examples than could be listed here, but this is a good "starter set" to get us going. We will examine a range of common issues that regularly block people from being even more effective and explore some thoughts on what you can do to work around the hitch.

I will provide examples of real-life situations that required workarounds and extract lessons from them. You will also see some workarounds that could have worked, that should have worked, but that wound up biting the dust anyway.

A Word of Caution

In our definition of workarounds, we noted that in the software world, workarounds are commonplace but also tend to be fragile. Increasing pressure to perform can cause some software workarounds to break down. While temporary workarounds can lead to the development of more permanent solutions, keep in mind that more often than not, workarounds are temporary solutions that may not stand the test of time. Much as with a jury rig in sailing (creation of a temporary mast when the real mast breaks) or the old country notion of holding something together with "chewing gum and baling wire," temporary fixes are likely to break down over time.

The caution here is that while you will certainly need to develop some workaround strategies from time to time, if you become overly reliant on them, you may wind up being perceived as someone who just doesn't fit in. That could be a good thing, but it could also be career limiting, depending on the circumstances. For example, if you deem a particular person, group, or process to be troublesome, you may concoct some clever workarounds that can be helpful; however, if you persist in dodging the person, group, or process rather than addressing the underlying issue, you may acquire a reputation for being difficult yourself!

The fact that you are sincerely trying to get something important done doesn't mean everyone else is going to appreciate your efforts or your sincerity. Some people will prefer to keep doing things the way they have been done before, simply out of convenience. For them, it's easier and less demanding to repeat an old process, even if it's not the best. Others may be concerned that your workarounds will show them up in some way. People don't like to be shown up, especially if they can't see a way to catch up.

You may even encounter the apparently productive types who are constantly busy to the point of being overwhelmed. Being overwhelmed and constantly busy can be a tactic to avoid taking on more meaningful or challenging work, and these superbusy types will require their own workaround strategies.

In *Workarounds That Work,* you will learn tools, systems, practices, and processes that make important initiatives easier to accomplish. Sometimes these workarounds will require additional effort, but not because the task or desired result takes superhuman skill. The additional effort comes because in order to effect the workaround, you may have to do some extra work, or even someone else's work, so as to get yours moving. That may not seem "fair," but it may be just how it is. If you put the weight on "fairness" over "productivity," you may come dangerously close to being known as one of those "that's-not-my-job" kind of workers.

HOW I GOT HERE FROM THERE

You may be wondering what qualifies me to write this book. Excellent question, really. I began my career in the mid-1970s as an educational psychologist, specializing in group dynamics and how teams form and perform. Throughout the '70s, I worked on the training side of things, building a personal development company that grew by word of mouth from a spare bedroom to 34 countries around the world. David Allen, author of the bestselling classic *Getting Things Done*, joined me in 1980, and we became partners in the development of leading-edge thinking about how to accelerate productivity for both individuals and organizations. Together, we worked hard on helping large organizations get more efficient and effective in hitting their goals and objectives, primarily by helping individuals "get things done." It soon became clear that whereas companies can come up with apparently fine strategies, goals, and plans fairly easily, it's a whole different ball game when it comes to executing those strategies and plans.

By the early 1990s, I was concentrating primarily on the execution of strategy in large organizations. Andersen Consulting, known today as Accenture, recruited me as an associate partner in its global change strategy think tank, where we focused on the people, process, and strategy components of change leadership. I left Andersen at the turn of the new millennium and have continued to work with management teams in companies of all sizes, focusing on how to help people and teams become even more effective in executing meaningful performance objectives.

Along the way, I have learned that there are several keys to success, one of which is the ability to work with and work around difficult situations, people, processes, and bureaucracies. The thrust of this book is how to overcome difficult challenges without adding to the difficulty yourself. My clients include Fortune 500 companies ranging from firms in aerospace and biotechnology to health care and financial services. That's quite an array, to be sure, and yet they all have something in common: regardless of company type or setting, people often need to find workarounds when something or someone gets in the way of being productive and generating meaningful results.

THE AIRLINE AND THE BLIZZARD

In January 2010, I was working with David Allen and a senior client team on a set of strategic realignment initiatives. David and I were both scheduled to arrive at the client's site in Louisville, Kentucky, one morning. It was the middle of a particularly cold and stormy season, and we both encountered blizzard conditions and significant weather delays on our trips the evening before the meeting. I flew in from the West Coast through Chicago, and thanks to some great support from United Airlines, other than changing planes a few times, I didn't have much of a problem. At least, not compared with what David had to go through. We both eventually set foot at the client's office the next morning; however, David had to employ a couple of very creative workarounds to get there.

David was flying from Los Angeles through Dallas, and his fun started with a significant delay out of Los Angeles. Although he, too, had access to great customer support, American Airlines informed him that there just weren't any flight options that would get him to Louisville until late the next morning, regardless of carrier or connecting city. American's support desk was focused on the next available flights into Louisville, whereas David was focused on being in Louisville in time for that 7:30 A.M. meeting the next day.

What would you have done if you were stranded in Los Angeles and needed to be in Louisville by 7:30 the next morning? The client surely would have understood if David had just waited out the storms and arrived when he could. After all, what can you do about the weather?

This is where three workaround basics become operative. The first and most important issue: what is your *intention*? The second critical aspect is your willingness to assume *control* of whatever you can that will move you forward. Once you are clear on your intention and have taken control of what you can, you then face the third element: how to *influence* others to go along.

Given that we may not be able to control the weather, and we probably can't influence it either, many of us would have settled for "doing our best." If it were just about "doing our best," I'm pretty sure waiting out the storm would have sufficed. David was focused on a heck of a lot more than simply "doing his best," though. His intention was to be there for the client—on time and ready to go.

Obviously, being there on time and ready to go is quite different from just doing your best. David was determined to find a workaround. With a clear intention firmly in mind, he Googled the weather conditions and driving routes to see if there was some city that might get him within driving distance of Louisville. St. Louis stood out as the most viable option, even though it's some-where between 263 and 354 miles from Louisville, depending on which route you drive.

He got back on the phone with American. Sure enough, they had one last flight heading to St. Louis. While boarding the plane, he arranged to pick up a rental car on arrival. Once he landed, he selected the best route given the conditions. Seven hours later, he was in Louisville. We both walked into that meeting at 7:30 A.M. as though nothing had happened, one of us a bit more refreshed than the other. The client was none the wiser—just well served.

Sometimes the challenge will be fairly simple and quite com-mon, not unlike the weather delays people encounter just about every day. As with the trip to Louisville, you may come up against someone who is doing his or her job, technically speaking, but not really doing the ultimate job. These kinds of situations require workarounds that work, and many will require you to take the initiative to reach a workable solution.

More complex concerns impinge when we start to think about challenges inherent in the effort to interface with colleagues, other teams, or even senior leadership. Issues often spring from mis-aligned silos, conflicting priorities, or bureaucratic internal pro-cesses. You may be caught up in apparently meaningless meetings, belabored by glacial consensus processes, or run ragged in endless fire drills.

My challenge will be to dig into a number of common situations that can be especially difficult and suggest workarounds that avoid blaming the other guy or putting someone on the spot. One part of this process will be conceptual, and the other part very practical. This book is designed to help you bridge the two and construct your own workarounds that are workable in your situation. Remember that as frustrating as it can be when you are confronted with road-blocks, especially internal roadblocks, it is rare that any person, team, or organization is actually plotting against you. If we come at other parties as though they are being intentionally difficult, we may wind up pouring gasoline on the fire.

Challenges, roadblocks, and bureaucratic snafus are commonplace and sometimes just as egregious at their heart as they appear to be on the surface. Nonetheless, if we get stuck in complaining about the situation, the other guy, the organization, or the frustrations, we may be fated to become more part of the problem than the actual solution.

HOW YOU FRAME THE PROBLEM IS THE PROBLEM

One of my all-time favorite quotes comes from Henry Ford. He famously declared that "whether you think you can, or think you can't, you're right." If you believe you can, you will keep on working at it until you find a way. If you believe you can't, then you will probably give up before you even engage. When people subscribe to the "I can't" kind of thinking, they rarely see choices that are readily available to them. Although not all choices are perfect choices, and some are beyond your current skill or ability, it can be pretty amazing to see what you can discover by simply asking yourself what choices you have that could make a difference.

Another classic pieces of advice for making life better is also the title of a highly recommended book by W. Mitchell, *It's Not What Happens to You, It's What You Do About It*. Mitchell is a master of workarounds. In fact, he works workarounds most every day of his life. The short version of his story is that after having recovered from a horrific motorcycle accident in which he was burned over 65 percent of his body, losing not only his face but also all of his fingers, he then became paralyzed as a result of an airplane crash four years later. Can you imagine the workarounds that he must have faced? And still faces?

From his website, wmitchell.com:

Undefeated by a blazing motorcycle accident and a paralyzing plane crash four years later, he learned to take responsibility for the countless changes in his life. Whether coping with devastating burns over 65% of his body or being sentenced to life in a wheelchair, this once robust Marine firmly held on to his feisty nature and quick wit. It was "his" uphill journey and he was determined to maintain control, cope with the changes, and prosper. Without a doubt, Mitchell understands what it takes to rebuild and eventually reach the top. His life clearly illustrates his philosophy—that most limitations are self-imposed.

The way he frames his life today is reflected in this poignant quote from his website, "Before I was paralyzed there were 10,000 things I could do. Now there are 9,000. I can either dwell on the 1,000 I've lost or focus on the 9,000 I have left." That's a world-class example of the concept that "how you frame the problem is the problem" and the notion that the first workaround may be with your own thinking. Some people can stub a toe and spend all day complaining about how they are being slowed down. Mitchell finds himself in a wheelchair, disfigured, and instead makes the best choices he can to work around his "limitations."

In the chapters that follow, I will frame a number of problems as unexpected roadblocks or unintended detours on the way to positive outcomes. With practice, you may get pretty good at spotting potential roadblocks or detours before you even get going. With foresight, you may develop your workarounds before the problem even surfaces and keep them in your back pocket "just in case."

Problems avoided can be so much more fun than problems overcome. Unless, of course, you cherish the fight along the way!

ASSUME THE POSITIVE

Just about all workarounds start with you and your internal attitude, intention, and determination. If you bump into something in your organization that seems like a roadblock, it may be useful to consider that what now appears to be a hindrance might have originated as something helpful. If you look first for the original positive intent, you may discover a key to moving forward. If, instead, you frame the imposition as nothing but a mindless hindrance, you are unlikely to get very far.

Considering the possible positive intent may be part of what's required to discover a creative workaround. If the original intent was positive, perhaps the only issue is in the how, not the what.

Larry Senn, of Senn-Delaney Leadership, calls this attitude "assume innocence." When you assume innocence, or a positive intent, rather than annoyance and intentional obstruction, any number of creative options may surface as you seek a way forward.

Sometimes the only thing you will need to do is keep asking yourself a question like this: "What problem were they trying to solve when they came up with this roadblock?" Again, very rarely does anyone sit around trying to come up with roadblocks—it just seems that way sometimes.

We will take a look at some cumbersome decision processes that originally showed up because of significant financial exposure and risk to human life. If you run up against unwieldy decision or approval processes, asking yourself what positive intention might be behind the process may help you discover some creative workarounds—workarounds that not only work this time but also may form the basis for a new and more efficient process going forward.

If you find yourself being blocked by a specific person or another team, it may prove fruitful to ask yourself what the problem looks like from the other party's position. From there, you may find any number of workarounds—workarounds that not only help you get where you're going but help the others get what they need as well. In the process, you may realize that you can turn apparent adversaries into partners.

CHOICES OF CONTROL AND INFLUENCE

In this book, we will approach just about every challenging situation with the same initial sets of questions: What happened? What outcome would you like? and What could you do about it? There are two basic categories of choice: what you can do directly that doesn't require permission or approval from anyone else, and what you could do with approval, cooperation, or permission from someone else. We will call the first area a choice of control, and the second a choice of influence.

Note that, just as in the situations David and I faced getting to Louisville—even if the workaround is about an external set of circumstances—you will always have some choice about what you can control. That will almost always come down to your willingness to own the outcome and do what you can to produce the outcome you desire.

As I dig into the question of how to push through when something appears to be in the way, I will use examples taken from real clients, examining how individuals or teams managed to work around the various apparent roadblocks.

As Henry Ford so wisely suggests, if you think you can, you will likely find a way through. If you think you can't, then you are likely to give up before you even start. If you hang out blaming others for the roadblock, even if you're right, you still wind up stuck. The key is you: it starts with your attitude and willingness to find a solution and then carries on to what choices you can make on your own. If you can bring these two elements to the party, then you may ultimately encourage a whole lot of others to join as well.

1

It All Starts with You

Organizations form when someone has a good idea, experiences early success, and then needs help in order to deliver on the promise. Somewhere between a good idea and market success, most businesses run into the challenge of setting up a system that helps move things forward more efficiently.

As the organization grows, a dilemma appears. Sooner or later we all discover the need for reliable, repeatable processes or systems lest the wheel becomes the constant reinvention. Systems and processes, however, can become overly engineered and eventually create more headaches than they solve, resulting in extra layers of approval and sign-off, thus delaying progress.

Employees often resist processes for reasons ranging from not wanting to be cramped in their style to fears of repeating the kind of bureaucratic nightmares they have experienced in past jobs.

Recently, I was working with two different companies, one in the technology security business and another in health care information automation. Both were successful, with a history of innovation and rapid growth, and yet both were frustrated by the lack of efficiency that had crept into their businesses.

The technology security CEO put it this way: "We're a billion-dollar company with a 50-million-dollar infrastructure." This company manages by consensus. Pretty much everyone needs to be on board. When consensus is lacking, just about any project, market plan, or customer service initiative can easily be derailed. Even routine matters require meetings, study, revisions, more study, and then tentative exploration of the possibility.

Unless, of course, the CEO sees another "bright, shiny object," and off people go again down a track that will drastically redirect company energy and resources. The "bright, shiny object" phenomenon prevents them from thinking strategically beyond the latest and greatest idea, while also leaving a number of groups in the dust when directions change and they didn't get the memo.

The health care information company CEO had a markedly different take on things: "We hire the best and brightest, but still they lack common sense." In this culture, decisions of any consequence run through the CEO's office, because the CEO does not trust that even senior managers will make the right decisions. On the one hand, it's hard to argue with success—while not the largest in the field, the company is number one in its category and has been growing like crazy. On the other hand, it is now confronting the consequences of its rapid growth and success. Too much going on, too many people involved, and too many opportunities on the horizon—no one CEO can put that many fingers into that many pies.

How do these companies adopt processes that can be trusted and implemented without overwhelming the cultures they have built? Both CEOs recognized the need to improve the way they operate their companies, for reasons that include increasing efficiency as well as improving their ability to compete in broader markets. However, as we plumbed the issues and possible solutions, both became paralyzed with the fear of implementing new processes that would result in an overbureaucratization of their "fast, flexible, and nimble organizations."

In actuality, though, neither company is quite as fast, flexible, or nimble as it once was. The fact is that they now tend to stumble over what used to be simple things. Coordination among groups has become somewhere between difficult and nonexistent. Approvals either take forever or are granted swiftly only to be overturned a short time later.

Employees are beginning to express frustration with the roadblocks to getting things done. Middle managers are becoming increasingly fearful that their decisions will be second-guessed. The combination of frustration and fear leads people to slow things down even more in a multitude of ways. Some are forever looking for "buy-in" before moving; some simply dig in and focus on dozens of small tasks, enabling them to demonstrate productivity in terms of the number of things accomplished—not necessarily the important things, just ones that can be counted; some are taking their own initiative, finding ways to get things done despite the organization roadblocks.

This book will look at some of the sources of organizational roadblocks and offer suggestions that you can employ to get things moving, to overcome internal resistance, and to make a difference. Again, as you find yourself bumping into what appear to be roadblocks or resistance, it will be important to keep in mind that just about every hurdle initially showed up for an apparently good reason.

It's not as if a senior team of roadblock specialists convenes weekly to figure out what else it can do to make things more difficult. For example, lengthy decision processes often come into existence for reasons such as lowering risk or engaging multiple stakeholders. It's hard to argue with lowering risk or engaging employees, yet it's also hard to find the value in delays when something critical shows up.

Some workaround suggestions will be fairly low risk; others may require you to take a deep breath, make sure your résumé is in good shape, and forge ahead knowing that the outcome may not be what you hoped for. The larger, perhaps riskier suggestions involve big ideas, concepts, and philosophies, often centering on the roles of leadership and management. Some of these will be strategic in nature, addressing what you are doing and why you are doing it. The smaller, lower-risk suggestions will be mostly tactical, emphasizing how you go about getting things done, meeting milestones, or complying with internal process standards.

Some of the actions we will discuss will be individual in form, things that you can do on your own or that involve just you and one other person. Some may involve you and your team members, and others may involve coordination across multiple teams. I will address a range of issues, many of which will reflect the following paradox: nothing in this book works, and yet everything in the book can work. The real difference will be what you choose to make work, to apply, or to utilize. None of these are perfect ideas, but each can be perfected.

A particular paradox and challenge will appear over and over again: what works for you and what works for me may be different, even if the same basic concept is in play for both of us. What you can make work and what I can make work may depend on any number of variables. Rather than reading this book in search of perfect answers that work perfectly, look for ideas that you can apply in your own unique way, and perfect them in your own environment.

CONTROL, INFLUENCE, AND RESPOND

Let's start with a simple way of examining your work world, building on a form of strategic thinking popularized by Steven Covey.

Years ago, the leaders of a unit of our armed forces hired me to help them improve efficiency in their operations. As part of the background for the engagement, they cited a model featuring three concentric circles as a way of thinking about strategy (see Figure 1.1). The three circles represent everything in your environment: things you can directly control all on your own, things you may be able to change if you can influence the right folks, and those things that are truly external to you and to which you can only respond.

If you *control* what you can and *influence* where possible, then you are most likely to be as well equipped as possible to *respond* to external circumstances. Change, competitive threats,

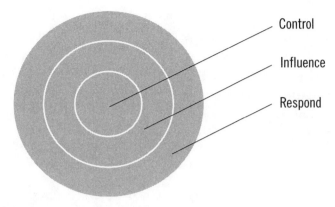

FIGURE 1.1

new technologies, and the like are just the way it is out there. The only thing you can do about the outside environment is respond. Winners are able to respond nimbly, with flexibility and adaptability, because they have figured out how to get things done, not just how to appease bureaucracies.

Imagine that the three layers represent your entire work life.

- **Control.** The inner circle contains all those things that you can control yourself, regardless of what others may say or do. While small, this circle does include choices you can make all on your own.

- **Influence.** The second layer relates to those areas of performance where you may be able to be impactful, but you require the approval, cooperation, support, or agreement of another. There may be many more areas here where you could imagine improvement, but it's not just up to you.

- **Respond.** This outer layer represents the rest of life. Turning again to the example of the weather, you can't really do anything about the rain other than decide how you respond. You can stay indoors, put on a raincoat, use an umbrella, or just decide that getting wet is OK. This is where most of life takes place: competitors do what they do, the economy moves the way it moves, and change just happens.

However, if you have prepared well by controlling what you can and influencing where possible, you should be able to respond or adapt to changing conditions that surround you in a much nimbler and more deft way. All kinds of people spend too much energy fretting about that environmental layer, where they can neither control nor influence the outcome. Contrary to conventional wisdom, where we get in trouble has less to do with what happens in the outer layer and much more to do with how well we manage the inner two circles.

Another common approach, which we will address in more detail later, takes the form of people trying to influence someone or something by complaining and finding fault with others. Even when the complaints about others are well founded, most complainers wind up being dismissed by management as "whiners." That's because the whiner-complainer rarely takes responsibility for his or her own role in the current situation or how to make it better. It's almost always someone else who needs to change.

The most important place to begin is right in the middle—that apparently small circle where you actually have control.

INTENTION VERSUS METHOD

If you allow yourself to lose sight of your purpose or intention, you will be unlikely to find a way through and will instead become overly focused on the hurdle in front of you. Once you clarify your intention and commit to it, you may begin to discover multiple ways to get there.

In the Introduction, I described David Allen's flight delay problems and how he worked around them. If he had glumly focused on the "insurmountable" problem of that uncontrollable variable, the weather, he would not have found his way to that meeting in Louisville. However, once focused on the positive outcome, his brain was able to step beyond the obvious and start the search for options.

We call this the distinction between intention and method. For every intention, there are multiple methods that may get you there.

In the Louisville example, many people would have been stumped by the lack of choices of airplanes going to Louisville. That's because their focus would have been on the method of travel rather than the intention of being there on time.

What do you do when the options come down to unattractive and even less attractive? That depends on a combination of your intention and your commitment. If the intention is sufficiently clear, as it was in this case, then you simply have to ask yourself if you are fully committed to the outcome.

There's an old saying from the early days of the personal growth movement that applies here: *99 percent is a bitch, 100 percent is a breeze.* I first heard this in 1973 when I attended a personal growth workshop. I suspect the concept, if not the actual phrase, goes so far back that no one really knows where it came from. With a 99 percent commitment, David might or might not have made it to Louisville. He might have called it a day in L.A. or a night in St. Louis. He might even have made it all the way to Louisville.

Even if he had made it that far, though, what state of mind would he have been in on arrival? If David had been operating from the 99 percent level, I suspect he would have been somewhere between exhausted and grumpy. At the 100 percent level, he showed up fresh, alert, and enthused. Not only was he thrilled to be working with this superb client, but also he could take deep satisfaction in the result he produced and the creativity he exhibited to get there.

RESPONSE-ABILITY

Fritz Perls, the founder of gestalt therapy, coined the term *response-ability*. The way to apply this concept to your own life is as follows: whenever you encounter a roadblock of any kind, look to yourself first. I suggest that in just about any situation, your ability to respond (*response-ability*) will be a function of your ability to *control* what you can, to *influence* what you can, and to simply *respond* to the rest.

As situations arise that require some form of workaround, consider what is within your own power to control, something you can do without needing to enlist anyone else in order to make a difference. No matter what the situation or circumstance, you will always have some choices in the matter, the foremost of which is how you choose to respond: your response-ability.

As you look for options, you will need to address at least two pieces to the puzzle: available responses measured against your ability to exercise those responses.

Sometimes people get into difficulty by declaring defeat— "There's nothing I can do about this." "It's hopeless." "Damned if I do, damned if I don't." As Henry Ford noted, if you believe you can't do anything, you won't even try. As stated in the Introduction, how you frame the problem is the problem. If you tell yourself there's nothing to be done, there may be available choices or responses that you simply don't see because of your mental attitude.

On the other hand, you may perceive numerous responses to any particular roadblock and recognize that one of them is the absolute best. It's the most elegant, most direct, and all-around perfect workaround. Except for one possible fly in the ointment: what if this perfect workaround response is something for which you are not currently skilled, trained, or prepared?

If it's a capability question, two courses are open. In some cases, you may be better off taking a less elegant solution that gets you through the immediate workaround challenge. In other cases, those in which the situation is likely to arise again, you may need to acquire the skill or training necessary to execute the more complex or elegant workaround. It may take more time and effort to develop the capability for this more elegant workaround, but investing that time and effort may in turn pay dividends when the same issue arises again in the future.

In any situation, you will have a range of responses and a range of abilities to tap. What makes one person effective and another less so may come down to how they frame the problem and how they perceive their ability to respond. If you need to get someone else on board, your first step is to look to anything you can handle on your own, your personal response-ability, before trying to enlist the other person. By taking control of what is truly yours, you will be in a much more powerful and influential position when you reach out to influence the choices someone else may need to make. At this point, you will finally be in the best position to respond effectively to outside circumstances, even those that seem out of your control, like the weather.

ACCOUNTABILITY: OWN THE GOAL, OWN THE PROCESS

In a way, accountability brings us back full circle, in that intention, commitment, response-ability, and accountability all support one another. In many respects, effective workarounds begin and end with accountability. You might have already experienced the conundrum of having established what you thought was a clear intention, committed to it 100 percent, and still come up short. An accountability mind-set asks the question, "What was my role in this outcome?" It may also ask, "What's my role in the solution?" This mind-set recognizes response-ability but stops short of blaming yourself—or anyone else, for that matter. Accountability is simply a way of owning the outcome, recognizing what's in front of you, and then taking the next best step you can.

Perhaps you have noticed that blame, complaint, and ducking accountability or response-ability have become somewhat commonplace in our daily lives. Not-my-fault and not-my-job attitudes abound out there. Given that many of us have encountered managers who punish mistakes rather than encourage learning, it is understandable that blame and finger-pointing have become so familiar. Not very effective, but understandable.

When you encounter problems in your job, it will serve you much better in the long run if you ask yourself how you could have been better prepared so that these kinds of obstacles are avoided next time around. Reverting to complaints or blame will drain off a considerable amount of your power to make choices and your ability to influence others.

IT ALL STARTS WITH YOU

Remember, the place to begin thinking about workarounds may just be with you! One of my favorite simple but telling questions is: *What could you do that would make a difference in your job that requires no one's approval, cooperation, support, or agreement other than your own?*

Think about your own job for just a minute. Try answering that simple question and see what you come up with. If you can discover wasteful exercises or processes within the company you work for, ask yourself what wasteful processes or exercises you have of your own. Are you late producing documents, deliverables, or other work products simply because you put tasks off, take too much time, or perhaps are a bit disorganized? If so, what can you do to become more efficient? What would happen if you got a bit more organized, planned your work just a bit better, or otherwise did what you could to improve? The simple answer is that you may get more work done, with a little less stress, and possibly with a bit more appreciation from others. You may even find that by making things easier on yourself, you also make things easier on someone else.

HOW IT WORKS

As we assess the various roadblocks to performance, we will identify several kinds of tips. Some will be more strategic in character, asking you to consider what you are trying to get done and why. Some will be more tactical, directed instead to how you will accomplish the result or complete the project.

Along the way, you will be asked to think about the tasks ahead and divide each into three areas of thought and action. Obviously, the best way to start is by exploring the control question: What could you do on your own that will make a difference? From there, the question concerns what you could do if you had agreement, support, cooperation, or approval and how you might influence those who would need to come along. Finally, you consider how handling the two inner circles of control and influence will enable you and your organization to respond more effectively to your business environment.

RISK, REWARD, AND MOVING FORWARD

As you will discover, many of the workarounds that you can employ are basically stealthy ones. That is, no one is likely to notice what you did differently, but people may notice that things are moving better. Even if no one else is aware of the change, at least you will be. One of the chief benefits of this approach lies in the improved quality of experience you will find in your job along with your enhanced ability to overcome obstacles and get important work done.

In addition to getting something done, you are likely to enjoy the fruits of increased job satisfaction, less stress, and a fuller sense of control. Even if no one else observes the extra effort you took to move something along, you will still reap the dual rewards of accomplishment and an improved job experience. Then again, you are also likely to uncover areas where significant improvement can take place, but without sufficient air cover, you are in danger of raising the political hackles of another group or of someone more senior than you or otherwise exposing yourself to the whims of corporate politics.

We have all heard the sage advice for surviving corporate politics: choose your battles wisely. You won't win all the time, and losing the wrong battle could be somewhere between career limiting and career ending. When your efforts are managed well, you can execute some valuable workarounds that not only will improve your job performance but also may establish you as someone to watch as you build on your record of success.

WORKAROUND QUESTIONS

In each chapter, you will find powerful workaround questions that will help you push through any of the roadblocks that are standing between you and your professional goals. Let's start by considering the following questions, which are intended to provide a more practical context for you as you read the chapters to come:

1. Where do you see room for improvement within your job, team, department, or business?

2. How clear are the goals and objectives where you work?

3. What kinds of communication issues do you see on the job?

4. How often do people encounter problems and devote more effort to placing blame than to fixing the problem?

5. Do various groups, teams, or departments seem to work in isolation when collaboration would be more useful?

6. How easy or difficult is it for your organization to arrive at a decision?

7. Do you encounter pockets of arrogance or "know-it-all" thinking that get in the way of improvement?

8. How effective are the meetings that you attend?

9. Do projects get delayed as people work to gain buy-in or consensus?

10. How efficient and effective is the e-mail system in your organization?

11. How effective versus bureaucratic are the processes in your organization?

12. Does your organization get bogged down trying to get to perfect solutions?

13. Are you just plain overwhelmed by the amount of work you have on your plate?

2

Getting the
Right Things Done

C hange keeps happening. Perhaps you have noticed. Sometimes change is welcome, and other times it is something
feared or dreaded. Change can come in all sizes, ranging
from the gargantuan to the relatively minor. It can be strategic in
form ("We are now going to enter a new line of business"), or it
can be relatively tactical ("Here's our new sales model"). It could
stem from an unanticipated problem (the customer is upset
because the order arrived wrong), it could come from installation
of a new computer system, or it could show up as a disaster
requiring an emergency response. More often than not, though,
change is simply something that is unexpected and brings with it
a lot of work.

In the corporate world, when things change, the usual mantra
goes something like, "Don't just sit there; do something!" Even if
you are a one-person shop, you have probably experienced the
phenomenon. Something unexpected happens, and some part of
you gets anxious, sure that you need to get busy and *do something*.
What's wrong with doing *something*? you may ask. Nothing,
really—as long as you can answer a more important question:

Does the something you are doing actually matter? In other words, should you join the fire drill or look for some kind of workaround?

As soon as you jump onto the "do something" bandwagon, you risk just doing something instead of doing the right things. Part of doing something meaningful involves knowing what you should stop doing so that you have room to do what matters most. If you are already busy, how are you going to respond when the next change shows up and you are faced with adding even more tasks to your already overflowing plate?

WHEN THE STATUS QUO GOES UP IN FLAMES

I once had a consulting client in Michigan, a company that manufactured car parts. The company had an aligned set of goals, and every manager and supervisor had his or her own comprehensive lists of tasks aimed at achieving those goals.

A couple of months after we finished the engagement, the company had a gas line rupture, and its main facility went up in flames overnight. Fortunately, no one was injured. As I was watching a news report about the crisis, my phone rang. It was the CEO of the manufacturing company. He told me that as soon as the fire broke out, the management teams began assembling at a hotel across a field from the now burning plant.

Each team had its lists of tasks linked to everything from key customers and product groups to key projects and next actions. Each team quickly reviewed what was on its plate and ran through a basic triage exercise to determine what needed to be addressed right away and what could wait. By midnight, the staff had a list of customers who were going to be impacted and began to put together a response plan to cover customer needs. By 3:00 A.M., they had identified alternative sources within their own system as well as from competitors, and they began putting together a plan to get needed materials to their customers. By 9:00 A.M., they had contacted their customers and competitors, confirmed the level of need, and begun arranging alternative supply choices.

By noon, the company had its emergency plan in place to fulfill immediate customer needs. The senior team then turned its attention to planning for longer-term supply options, while another team set about the planning process for a new plant.

DIRECTIONALLY CORRECT VERSUS PERFECTIONALLY CORRECT

Instead of asking, "What should I do?" the question should become, "What's the right thing to do?" By "right," I don't mean right compared with wrong; rather, I mean what would be *directionally* correct. Are you taking action that will reasonably move the project forward? Will the action you take help resolve the issue at hand?

My good friend and former partner David Allen (*Getting Things Done*) has long counseled that you don't need to know all the steps in a project in order to get started. At a minimum, you do need to know the desired outcome and an appropriate next step. As long as you know the outcome and the next step, you can make progress.

To be effective, matching an outcome with a next step requires some thinking and a modicum of planning. When management decides to change directions, and the orders go out to get busy, rarely is there an accompanying order to stop doing something else. A smart manager realizes that herein lies an opportunity for making a real difference in not only *how* things get done but also *which* things get done. One of the singularly most important things management can do when issuing the "get busy, do something" dictum is to actually think about what no longer needs doing.

For example, if you are going to start deploying a new quality-control process, are there old processes that need to be abandoned? If you are implementing a new data-tracking system, are you still tracking old data that no longer matter? If the company is taking on a whole new strategic direction, you may need to add all kinds of new goals and plans, but you also need to identify old goals and plans that should be taken down. After all, if people are already up to their ears in work, and someone tells them to add something to the mix, sooner or later either they will break down, the system will break down, or both.

FEELING GOOD ABOUT GETTING THINGS DONE

For those who already feel as though they are working perhaps too hard, allow me to ask two seemingly dumb questions: Have you ever exercised? And, have you ever cleaned a refrigerator by accident?

How Work Is like Exercise

If you've ever engaged in a decent exercise session, how did you feel when you were finished? Sure, at first you might've been a bit tired, but once your respiratory rate stabilized, how did you feel? Unless you had just finished something truly grueling, such as a marathon, you probably noticed that within a few minutes of finishing, you felt pretty good. In fact, most of us wind up feeling better than when we started, as though we had more energy. Logically, that can't be the case. After all, you just finished expending considerable energy, burning calories. Surely you must now have less energy than when you began. Right?

Logic notwithstanding, most of us will feel as if we have even more energy. Why? Because humans are programmed to produce energy by burning energy. Once you get the system in motion, the body starts to notice that it is burning energy. As available gas in the gas tank goes down, the body starts to burn fat (stored energy) so that it can continue to fuel the engine. Even when you stop exercising, the body keeps on producing energy for some time.

Obviously, this won't go on forever if you don't stop, replenish, and rest from time to time. Nevertheless, the salient point is that you produce energy by expending energy.

The same is true regarding work, with a couple of minor differences. On the work front, many of us have tasks to perform that lack the kind of clarity found in exercising, especially in terms of a defined purpose, outcome, and deliverable. If you can assign yourself these attributes for your work, you may notice that you actually start to feel the same kind of response as when you exercise. Completing a task takes some effort, but it also produces its own reward. If others notice, comment, or acknowledge your contribution, so much the better. Either way, simply getting things done that you set out to accomplish will begin to produce something akin to the exercise phenomenon—the more you get done, the more inclination you will have to get even more done.

If you've ever had to just sit around all day and do nothing, you might have noticed how tiring doing nothing can be. Doing something is, of course, better than doing nothing. However, it's even better when you have a defined purpose, outcome, and deliverable by which to measure the fruits of your labor.

Cleaning a Refrigerator by Accident

Perhaps you were sitting at home once, reading a book or watching TV, and you decided you wanted a snack. As you were grazing in the fridge, you noticed some leftovers that had become something like a science experiment—kind of green and growing fuzzy things that didn't look all that safe. So, you toss the science experiment into the trash, and then curiosity takes over. What else is in there that no longer belongs?

Pretty soon you're opening jars, discovering more fuzzy growing things, disposing of old veggies, and generally getting rid of products that should have been thrown out long ago. Then, as you stand back admiring your work, you notice the dry, brown crusty stuff that used to be a liquid. Out comes the sponge, the drawers hit the sink, and without much thought or real effort, the refrigerator is clean again. From there, you probably even took that sponge to the countertops and did a bit of kitchen cleaning as well.

The simple act of going to grab a quick snack led to cleaning a refrigerator, which led to a sense of accomplishment, which led to even more cleaning and to even more accomplishment. I seriously doubt that you would have had "Clean refrigerator" on your to-do list, and yet something inspired you to dive into a job that ordinarily would have been akin to drudgery.

You Feel Great When You Get Finished

What do exercise and refrigerators have to do with workarounds? In the world of work, unfinished tasks, projects, and objectives all hold a certain amount of your mental energy, attention, or focus. When you get something done, whatever energy, attention, or focus you had invested in that incomplete item is released and becomes available to you. In a way, incomplete goals, objectives, projects, or tasks are like the fat you carry in your body. They're both stored energy, and both can be released simply by your getting going. As you complete your unfinished work, you generate more energy, which in turns makes it easier to accomplish even more.

The refrigerator example shows what can happen when you come up against a real-world situation that is beyond what you consider to be the normal bounds of acceptability. When you compared how that refrigerator looked with how it was supposed to look, you quickly moved into action. The old, incomplete tasks clogging up your mental refrigerator become even more compelling. The only person who can identify and do anything about these kinds of "science experiments" on your task list is you. That's why you have to clean out everything from your mental refrigerator to your in-box.

Just as with exercising, you feel great when you get finished.

YOU'RE NOT OVERWHELMED; YOU'RE EMPLOYED

In the 30 years I have been helping organizations execute their strategies, I have had the opportunity to help a whole lot of folks up and down the organization get better organized so that they can get more things done. In today's world, the constant mantra seems to be about doing more with less, getting more work accomplished with fewer resources and reduced head count. I understand the necessity for this kind of thinking. I also contend that we can get there without driving everyone crazy.

As people make lists of all the items on their plates, the good news is that they get a whole lot of stuff out of their minds and onto sheets of paper or electronic files. The bad news is that the sense of dread about everything that needs to be done can become overwhelming. That's because some part of you thinks you are actually supposed to get it all done. *Now.*

Big problem.

The first counsel I offer is that having more to do than you can get done is actually welcome news. You may ask, what's so wonderful about having more to do than can readily be done? It's called having a job. You're employed. By definition, a job means having more things to do than can get done. That's why it's not a *temporary* job. Things keep showing up that need to get done, and you were hired to help. Not to get everything done, but to keep everything moving.

That said, having seen thousands of lists over the years, I have noticed that people inside organizations can have all kinds of entries on their lists that no longer matter. These are simply legacy actions that might have made sense way back when but that no longer have much value. Keeping them around is akin to carrying an extra 20 pounds of fat on your body. It's tiring, to say the least, and it slows you down in any number of ways. These are the folks who are on the road to becoming overwhelmed and burned out. It's notable that the only people who become overwhelmed and burned out are the ones who actually care! They would prefer to be engaged in meaningful work, getting things done that matter, and to have someone notice the results of their efforts.

What you need to know is that being overwhelmed and burning out do not have as much to do with all the things on one's plate as with how little those items matter. No one relishes the thought of going to work today to produce another load of "same old, same old." That's just shorthand for "I have no idea why this matters; they just pay me to do it." Sooner or later a load of inconsequential activity can, well, just overwhelm you. Now that you know that, what can you do? How can you work around that sense of dread and of being overwhelmed?

You can start by taking a comprehensive look at the list of things you have on your plate and then simply asking yourself three questions: "Why is this on my plate?" "What difference does it make?" "Who would notice if I didn't do it?" We'll return to these three questions shortly. For the moment, consider what might happen if you identified a number of items on your plate that really don't make much difference. How much time and energy would you free up if you could circle those low-value tasks and just drop them altogether?

START, STOP, CONTINUE: THE ANTIDOTE
TO BEING OVERWHELMED

If people are already up to their ears in things they need to get done, how are they going to create room for all the new stuff without going completely crazy? All types of organizations seem to be caught in some kind of schizophrenic bind: on the one hand, they want to encourage a proper work-life balance, and on the other, they want to have more work performed by fewer people consuming fewer resources.

This feat can actually be accomplished with a slight twist on how you articulate the goal. Is it about having fewer people get more things done, or is it about getting more of the right stuff done? Is it a simple scorecard tracking actions and tasks, or is it a more sophisticated scorecard tracking meaningful results accomplished? Obviously, the primary goal should comprise meaningful results.

If an organization is going to efficiently change directions, adopt new strategies, or simply set new goals, a worthwhile exercise would be to ask three basic pruning questions:

- Based on the new direction, strategy, or goal, what should we *start* doing?

- Based on the new direction, strategy, or goal, what should we *stop* doing?

- Based on the new direction, strategy, or goal, what should we *continue* doing?

It's that middle question that matters most. Are there tasks, procedures, processes, or systems in place that no longer serve our current or future directions? There is evidence that organizations can free up as much as 20 percent of someone's time and effort by simply exercising the discipline to review what's already on people's plates and eliminate the stuff that no longer matters. It's a lot easier to get people following a new direction if the organization can create a little relief from the already mind-numbing amount of no-longer-meaningful work that awaits them.

So, what do you do if your management keeps adding to your plate without providing any relief?

How about reviewing your list of goals, projects, and tasks and matching them up to the new direction, goals, projects, and tasks coming down from on high?

If you do so, you can then triage the list into the three previously cited buckets:

1. **Start:** What should you start doing as a result of the new direction?

2. **Stop:** What should you stop doing as a result of the new direction? What no longer matters?

3. **Continue:** What should you continue to do that still matters?

Once you have reviewed your lists and matched them to current goals and regular support functions, you can then go to your manager and frame the conversation around being able to get more done and improving the odds of achieving critical goals. If you can proactively show improvement opportunities absent of whining or complaining, you may not only gain some relief for your own workload but also inspire others to do the same.

Imagine what would happen if the whole team wound up saving 20 percent of its time? Think anyone would notice or care that some tasks were eliminated? If we don't do something to create a little more space, to provide a modicum of relief from what's no longer meaningful, we will surely drive ourselves crazy accomplishing all kinds of things that no one will really notice.

In the mid-1980s, I found myself teaching a course for the plastics division at GE's storied Learning Center in Crotonville, N.Y., which has since been renamed the John F. Welch Leadership Development Center. GE was famous for having its most senior leaders spend time teaching relative new hires at Crotonville, and Jack Welch himself was the leading proponent of this practice.

The story goes that Jack Welch asked a version of the "Why is this on my plate?" question early on in his tenure as CEO of GE. Every day when he showed up at his office, there would be a fresh stack of z-fold computer printouts more than a foot high waiting for him. He asked one day, "What's this?" He was told, "That's your overnight worldwide sales and inventory report."

What? It's true: he was getting a report every day on what was sold globally, as well as how much was in inventory, right down to warehouse location, country by country, business unit by business unit. What value did this report have? None that he could see and none that anyone could explain, other than to say that his predecessor liked having it. So, he simply had it stopped. That freed up a small team of people who assembled it overnight. From there, he is said to have issued a dictum that if you were producing something for which you saw no apparent reason or value, you had permission to stop producing it and engage in a conversation about purpose, value, form, and substance.

This tactic is kind of like spring cleaning, only for office systems, procedures, and processes that have piled up. Oftentimes, you'll come across work that might have been meaningful early on and that has become embedded into the culture of the organization. As new goals, projects, and tasks show up, they are automatically added to the stack of things that people "need" to do.

Rarely does anyone question the necessity of keeping older methods, projects, or processes in place. After all, "that's just the way we do things around here."

Workaround: Let Go of the Old

A relatively easy workaround is to periodically question what's on your list of goals, projects, or tasks. Using the control-influence-respond model we addressed in the first chapter, you may find that simply asking three questions of yourself is enough to streamline what's on your plate. Start by reviewing your list of tasks, projects, or to-dos, and then ask these three questions about each item you have cited:

1. Who needs this done?

2. Why do they need it?

3. What difference will it make?

This is a handy little low-tech questioning process that may prove exceptionally valuable if done regularly—say, monthly. At a minimum, you should run through these questions whenever a new goal, direction, or strategy looms. If this is where we are headed, how do the things on my task list align with the new goal, direction, or strategy?

When I work with senior managers on implementing their strategies, I always like to ask a version of these kinds of questions. Just as trees need pruning in order to stay healthy, getting rid of the deadwood in your environment opens up room for growth. Practices, systems, and "ways of doing things" just seem to develop over time and stick around, much like the dead branch on the tree. Pruning old processes and methods can be a powerful act.

Enforcing Nonexistent Regulations

A good friend of mine has served as a director for the state of California under several governors, overseeing the distribution of funds to social services programs. Tim has all kinds of stories about systems and processes that need workarounds. One of my favorites: In his role, Tim was tasked with making certain that not-for-profit agencies received their funding and also followed appropriate state and federal guidelines. As part of the funding process each year, not-for-profit groups had to sign a contract that was 100 pages long, while finance officials audited both the state agency and the receiving groups to make certain everything was in compliance.

Sounds reasonable, doesn't it? Well, not to the not-for-profit groups. Working with the auditors on even a single item of potential noncompliance could suck up more than 40 hours of work. That's time they could have spent delivering services. Instead, they were struggling to comply with rules and regulations. Tim sat down with representatives of one of the not-for-profit groups that had complained to him. As they pored over the contract, Tim was stunned to learn that there were multiple clauses that existed without any apparent reason. There were even compliance clauses for laws that were no longer on the books!

You would think that an obvious workaround would be to disregard those useless clauses. However, pity the poor recipient who chose not to follow the nonexistent regulations. Even though the laws were no longer in force, noncompliance could result in anything from withheld funding to demands to have already-spent funds sent back. Yikes!

Once Tim understood the scope of the problem, he met with a team of staff members, auditors, contract officers, and principals from a couple of not-for-profit groups. They reviewed the contract line by line, paragraph by paragraph. As a result of this rather simple but tedious workaround, old regulations were removed. Requirements that no one understood were investigated, and many of them were also dropped over time. The final product was a contract that shrank from 100 pages to 20 pages. A whole lot of wasted time and energy was recovered for the funding recipients as well as for the three state departments involved in overseeing the distribution of funds.

WORKAROUND QUESTIONS

There are several layers to the workaround required for getting things done and responding to change. If the issue is managing your sense of being overwhelmed, the workaround can be as straightforward as organizing what's already on your plate so that you can make better choices about where to direct your efforts. If the issue is preparing for a planned change, then the workaround still involves knowing what's on your plate, so that you can determine what needs to stay and what can go, and then you can plan for what needs to be added.

Each area requires a variant of the start-stop-continue analysis. Before you can accurately analyze your choices, you need a complete list of what's on your plate right now. So, before going any further, make a comprehensive list of all items large and small that you are responsible for doing, including goals and objectives you are responsible for achieving.

Managing an Overwhelming Workload

1. Challenge each item on your list:
   - Why is this on my list?
   - What goal, objective, or management process does this support?
   - Does it still matter?
   - What would be lost if I stopped doing it?

2. Review your list of tasks that are no longer relevant with your boss for agreement.

3. Make a new, shorter list of only those items that matter.

Responding to Change

1. Review your list of things to do and goals to accomplish.

2. Map each item to goals and objectives that you are responsible for achieving.

    • Which items appear to be no longer relevant and can be dropped?

    • Which items link to current goals and processes that still need doing?

    • Which new tasks should become part of your response-ability for achieving new goals, objectives, or strategies?

3. Review this list and your underlying logic with your boss for agreement.

4. Finalize your new list, including goals, objectives, and tasks.

3

Misaligned Leadership and Unclear Direction

A great mentor of mine, Jeff Bowden, correctly foresaw an interesting niche in consulting: helping organizations translate new strategic directions into meaningful implementation plans. And not just plans, but the actual execution itself. Sometimes the single biggest problem in an organization is faulty leadership alignment. It could be that different leadership teams, on any level, are working at cross-purposes, or it could be that their goals conflict with each other. Sometimes conflicts are over turf and politics, sometimes they are personal, and sometimes each leader or team is doing what he or she thinks is best but without sufficient alignment and shared sense of direction.

Large organizations can be dysfunctional, or they can be crisply aligned and operationally excellent. In this chapter, let's look at the issue from the point of view of alignment and direction. After all, rarely does leadership sit around in endless meetings trying to devise new ways to make things difficult; it can just seem that way at times to people further down the food chain. What follows is a glimpse into the challenge, taken from my years in consulting with senior teams on the implementation of strategy—not the creation of strategy but the actual work required to implement the strategy effectively.

DOES MANAGEMENT KNOW WHERE WE'RE GOING?

How many times have you heard about frontline employees, those with actual customer contact or direct responsibility for delivering a product or service, who are frustrated by their management or by other groups when it comes to delivering a high-quality product or superior service? It's usually not for lack of great company vision statements promising to deliver "world-class service" and "superior value" to "delighted customers" that "exceeds expectations." We have all bumped up against "Dilbert" mission statements that fall flat.

If you work for an organization that promises the moon and can't get off the launching pad, how do you overcome internal challenges, obstacles, and other roadblocks if you actually do want to make a difference and get something done? To be fair, let's keep in mind that your company probably truly does want to deliver world-class service to delighted customers. It's just that senior management likely has no idea how frustrating it is to actually do that.

So, What's in the Way?

While there may be dozens of other candidates, in the following chapters we will discuss common practices that result in corporate roadblocks to achieving great results. For each of these internal roadblocks, a set of effective workarounds is offered. The discussion will include a handful of real-life examples, many of which involved several workarounds.

Perhaps the challenge to increased effectiveness can best be summed up with the old story about something that had to be done:

> An important job had to be done, and everybody was sure that somebody would do it. Anybody could have done it,

but nobody did it. Somebody got angry about that because it was everybody's job. Everybody thought that anybody could do it, but nobody realized that everybody wouldn't do it. It ended up that everybody blamed somebody when nobody did what anybody could have done.

A comment we hear in organizations just about every day intended to justify same-old-same-old thinking reprises the age-old theme of "that's just the way we do things around here." That posture leads sooner or later to "that's not my job" thinking. From there, it's a short slide into the inferno of "check your brain at the door—they don't pay us to think around here."

Given that state of affairs, what do you do if you actually care—if you actually think, if you truly want to get something meaningful done?

CREATING ALIGNMENT

Let's take the example of Jack Bauer, from the television show "24." He's forever up against his own government's bureaucracy, one that is seemingly more interested in following procedures than actually preventing the terrorists from blowing up the world. Now, I realize that "24" is a stretch. Not many of us are dealing with saving the world from thermonuclear holocaust, and seldom will torture and assassination be in our tool kits.

All the same, I'll bet you can still recognize similar challenges in your own organization. You may see the way forward, and someone is quick to tell you that your idea just won't work or that the rules prevent it. If you haven't experienced this scenario where you work, perhaps you have friends who have been through this version of hell.

If you do recognize the challenge, then perhaps you need your own team of agents dedicated to rooting out the roadblocks, over-coming the obstacles, and getting things moving again. Maybe you will have to become an independent agent, your own Jack Bauer, working alone to get things done until the higher-ups start to notice.

Over the past three decades, I have worked with several major aerospace companies on how to improve their ability to attain the Holy Grail of government contract performance: meeting schedule, cost, and quality targets. As you might have noticed, the aerospace industry frequently bumps into situations that culminate in large cost overruns and late projects burdened with performance problems.

Here's how one aerospace engineer put it:

> If ever there were a textbook example of a dysfunctional organization where nothing gets done except under the table, it's the company I work for. My blood-and-guts approach is to ignore management and do what I think is right, at whatever personal consequence. We seem to have two kinds of effective managers here. They are polar opposites to each other and do things totally differently, yet both are fairly successful. We have the "politically correct" maverick who looks after personalities, feelings, and political positions, while the "covert operator" flies underneath the radar screen, maneuvering whatever it takes to get the job done. Both get things done when their organization is heavily stacked against them, both are highly imaginative, and both have a habit of "coloring outside the lines." Interestingly, neither style seems to make it to VP, precisely because they often do not agree with VPs that certain things are impossible.
>
> Quite frankly, much of my company is managed by executives who will happily tell you something won't work and will punish you if you prove them wrong. Seriously, people get punished for succeeding! Amazing, but true.

My oh my! Can you imagine what that culture must be like? Sounds as if someone needs to fine-tune the alignment in that organization . . .

Get Everybody on the Same Page

When I undertake a performance-improvement assignment for any size of organization, I like to begin with a meeting of the senior team. That team could be the executive committee of the entire corporation, or it could be the senior team charged with running a business unit, a manufacturing location, or a critical functional group. For our purposes, let's imagine we are sitting down with the seven members of an executive committee.

We start out with a brief introduction, stating that our purpose is to help the organization accelerate measurable and meaningful performance against critical strategic imperatives. From there, it goes something like this: "Ladies and gentlemen, please take out a sheet of paper and write down what you consider to be the mission, vision, or purpose of this organization."

I then collect those seven sheets of paper and read them back aloud. Fifteen years ago, it would have been highly unlikely that those seven statements bore much resemblance to one another. In today's world, in contrast, most groups can echo something pretty similar. I suppose that accomplishment has something to do with a combination of consultants and marketing departments who produce slogans engraved on walls and printed on name badges. That's a good thing.

The next request goes something like this: "Please take out another sheet of paper and write down what the top three strategic goals are for the coming 12 to 18 months."

This is where it gets interesting. Typically, adding up the responses on these seven sheets of paper will reveal an average of 18 answers to the question about the top three strategic goals. Seven people, three goals, 18 answers. Swell, huh? From there, it's a self-evident query to the assembled team: "If you have 18 answers to a question about the top three goals, is it any wonder you have so many disagreements about priorities, funding, resource allocation, head count, and so forth?"

The next telling question: "If you have that much differentiation sitting around this leadership team, what must it be like three layers down? How confident are you that if you could look over the shoulders of your key managers, you would see them working on what you consider the most critical tasks, projects, or goals?"

As you can imagine, this wake-up call tends to both get their attention and generate quite a bit of push-back. The Ops person says their focus is different from Sales, which is different from Finance, which is different from HR, and so on. "Of course we have different goals—we have different functions."

They may be correct, but they are not aligned. Even though they all share the same "vision," they each translate that vision according to the specific role or function that pertains.

Rather than examining corporate performance through the lenses of their respective functions or silos, what would it be like if they all could articulate the same three, four, or five critical goals that the organization needs to achieve in order to be successful? What if from there, each group, business unit, or functional area could articulate how its part of the business aligns to support those key organizational goals? What if each could articulate the goals, objectives, and key projects that its respective units need to achieve in order to stay on track, both as individual units and as a larger corporate entity?

Instead of dozens of priorities, they would have some five to seven truly critical priorities around which the organization could align. Granted, there are probably at least 20 to 30 other areas requiring attention, each having its own claim to being a priority. However, once you spend the time to clarify the critical few, you are likely to find that the critical few serve to drive the others.

I know this is what most organizations say they do, but it's not what happens much of the time. If any of this saga sounds familiar to you, try not to take it personally. It's a lot harder than it may seem to align a bunch of moving parts, especially when the metrics for each part tend to be more about the silo than the organization as a whole. In fact, most organizations struggle with how to find metrics that integrate corporate objectives with individual unit performance, much less cross-unit integration.

However, if we can get the senior leadership talking about this subject for even a few hours, we are likely to identify those critical few priorities that, if accomplished, will help drive the others at the same time. In fact, it's kind of like driving a car: the car has hundreds of moving parts, each critical, but you can organize them with a few key priorities, probably no more than six or seven.

For example, could you manage if you had information only on speed, fuel, the electrical system, and fluids coupled with the ability to control acceleration, direction, and braking? Even though all kinds of other things are going on, with just a few critical components to focus on, you can organize and manage your way down the road.

Make sense? Written this way, it probably does. So, what's the challenge, and how does it impact people up and down the organization?

If individual leaders lose sight of the larger purpose and vision, they will tend to become a bit myopic in their focus on unit performance. In extreme cases, unit performance can outstrip the larger goals of the organization. Oddly enough, the more myopic or narrowing of focus, the more the number of priorities is likely to grow.

CONFLICTING GOALS, PROCESSES, AND PRIORITIES

Could the frustration you feel in trying to get something done in your organization be traced to misaligned leadership? Are different groups marching toward different goals or to different performance drumbeats? Are you being measured on your ability to get something across the finish line, but you require the support, cooperation, or coordination of another group? If so, then you might have also encountered the situation in which the other person, department, or team recognizes the importance of your project, but it's just not on that party's performance radar screen; the boss of that area is measuring people based on something else altogether.

Working from the theory that happy career equals happy boss, it's hard to fault the other folks for paying attention to what makes their bosses happy. So, what do you do when these kinds of conflicts show up? Let's back up a couple of steps and revisit the notion of control, influence, and respond, which was introduced in the first chapter. Sometimes the biggest improvement opportunities start right at your own desk. On many occasions, I have seen apparently large organizational stumbling blocks virtually dissolve as a result of the exercise of asking three direct questions:

1. What needs improving around here and why?

2. What could you do that would make a difference that requires no one's permission other than your own?

3. What could you do that would make a difference that requires permission, cooperation, or approval?

If you apply these three questions to the real work you have in front of you, you may be pleasantly surprised to note how many issues dissolve simply as a function of how you answer the second question. I'll bet that you have a heck of a lot more power and control than you think you do. It's easy to fall into the trap of thinking that nothing will ever change in your arena, especially when you have seen well-intentioned people go down in flames when they tried to make some kind of meaningful difference. You needn't abandon hope, because question number two still contains considerable hidden power: simply by posing the question to yourself, you may discover a number of actions that you can take on your own that will help. Once you take the appropriate actions that you can, you will most likely rise in the perception of others—"Now, there's someone who is willing to act." As a result, you may be in a position to wield greater influence than those who merely complain. Even if no one else gets on board, by taking the actions that you can, you will make a difference, and at least one person is guaranteed to notice—*you*!

WORKAROUND QUESTIONS

Workarounds can vary from the rudimentary and tactical to the complex and strategic. Even at the most basic levels, it's important to keep in mind what your intention is in coming up with the workaround. Determining what the issue is and why it matters needs to come before charting what you can do and how you make it happen.

The following questions all build on the core focus areas of control and influence. If you have a specific issue that needs a workaround, you can apply this question string to that specific issue. You can also use the sequence to examine your job in general and perhaps discover areas that could be improved that have not previously shown up on your radar screen.

1. What around your workplace could be improved?

2. Why does it matter? (critical goals, improved performance, ability to produce results, etc.)

3. Who cares about this other than you?

4. What could you do to make a difference that requires no one's permission other than your own? (personal organization, project management, time management, meeting management, decision making, information sharing, etc.)

5. What impact would taking that action have on the situation?

6. What impact would taking that action have on how you perform your job?

7. What impact would taking that action have on someone else (a coworker, your own team or department, other teams or departments, customers, etc.)

8. How would the other person(s) notice?

9. If you improve what you can on your own, what else could be improved if you had permission, approval, cooperation, or support?

10. Who would need to be on board?

11. Why would it matter to them? To their management? To the organization?

12. How would their own jobs or experience of their jobs improve if they took action?

13. How does having taken your own independent action help them take theirs?

14. How can you support them in the process?

15. How would taking this approach to improvement help you better respond to customer, supplier, or competitor situations?

4

How You Frame the Problem Is the Problem

How many problems do you stumble across every day? What do you do about them? How often is the problem a function of what someone else did or didn't do? Albert Einstein had something to say about the problem of problems. You might have heard this one before: "No problem can be solved from the same level of consciousness that created it." The example in Chapter 2 of compliance officers auditing outdated regulations is a case in point. Asking compliance-control people to adjust compliance procedures is likely only to generate more compliance procedures. Problem solving requires a certain kind of imagination; problem prevention requires an entirely different ability. Einstein had another interesting take on the subject: "Intellectuals solve problems, geniuses prevent them."

UNLOCK YOUR INNER GENIUS

Take a look around you. Do you see anything that didn't exist 5,000 years ago? I know: what a dumb question. But go ahead, look around. Do you see phones, computers, or electric lights?

Perhaps you see airplanes, cars, or trains. No doubt you can see even more cool and exotic things that weren't around 5,000 years ago.

Or did they?

Let's take that computer or cell phone you probably have handy. Even more cool: what if you're reading this text on a Kindle or Nook or iPad or some other newish technology? Was there anything required to build that computer, cell phone, or Kindle that didn't already exist 5,000 years ago? The silicon was there; the oil that became the plastics was there; the copper or titanium and anything else you can name—everything was there, just waiting for someone to have the imagination necessary to come up with the idea that would require correctly assembling those basic parts. Sometimes all it takes is for someone with vision to frame an idea differently. Imagination and creativity often stem from someone's looking at a familiar problem but with a different frame of reference.

HOW ARE YOU FRAMING THE PROBLEM?

In many respects, the only real workaround you will ever need may just be contained in this one simple phrase: *how you frame the problem is the problem.* When something happens to us, we frame it in one way or another before we can make any choices about how to respond. Even before we can set an intention, we need first to put the issue, problem, challenge, roadblock, hurdle, or opportunity into some kind of context.

You probably are familiar with the now clichéd observation that the Chinese character for *threat* is the same as the Chinese character for *opportunity*. Well, the reason clichés exist is that they've been proved to be true, or at least apparently true, by so many for so long. Anyway, if we frame a problem as a threat, we respond in some fashion ranging from defensiveness to aggression. If, instead, we frame the problem as opportunity, we may start to uncover options that were not previously apparent. The options might have always been available to us, but our mental framework might have blocked us from perceiving them.

As I stated earlier, the first workaround in just about any circumstance may be the need to work around your own self. If you frame yourself as the victim of circumstances, ineffective processes, stubborn counterparts, misaligned leadership, poor communication, or any number of other external situations, you may never manage to move, succeed, or experience the kind of satisfaction you would hope for on the job—or just about anywhere else, for that matter.

We have much to gain as well as to lose by how we frame our challenges. Frame yours well!

NATURAL FOODS, DELICATESSENS, AND GROCERY STORES

My friend Irwin Carasso has always been an imaginative guy with a pretty positive outlook on things. When I asked him about his ideas on workarounds, he told me that the notion of labeling something a problem was both a "problem" to be worked around itself and a form of self-imposed limitation. He put it this way: "The very nature of labeling something as a problem automatically sets it up as a block to going forward, in a number of ways. I always chose to look at problems more like puzzles and had fun finding a more creative way to deal with them."

Irwin grew up in St. Augustine, Florida, and put in a lot of time working at his father's grocery store before heading off to Northeastern University in Boston. After a year or so at Northeastern, he decided to return to Florida and attend college there. By then, he had developed a solid preference for natural and organic foods, a category that was only beginning to emerge back in the late 1960s and early 1970s.

As he would tell you, Irwin has always been adept at finding ways to get something at a better price. Natural foods were expensive, and on a college budget, cheap was good. He was able to get his father to order some products for him using his grocery connections, which got him to thinking that others in the area might have a similar interest. He persuaded his father to let him set up a small rack in the store and try selling a few natural grocery and vitamin products. You get the drift, I'm sure. Irwin soon had much more shelf space devoted to selling high-margin products.

Based on how well Irwin was doing with a modest amount of space, his father agreed to loan him $15,000 to open a natural foods store in a new wholesale unit he was planning to launch. Irwin called the store Tree of Life. The store took off like crazy, and Irwin took out another loan, this time to expand into wholesale distribution of natural foods. He proceeded to contact a variety of other small players, and in time, Tree of Life became the nation's largest distributor of natural foods. Through Tree of Life, he soon was helping small companies such as Celestial Seasonings become major players, while also supplying little stand-alone stores such as Whole Food Store, located in New Orleans. (Yes, that Whole Food Store, which became the chain we now know as Whole Foods.)

Let's take a look back at the seminal events of Irwin's story. Here he is, living in St. Augustine, on a college kid's budget, with a taste for expensive, natural foods. By reframing his "problem" (expensive foods available only through specialty stores) as something to be solved, he exposed the puzzle called food distribution and began to solve it. His father's store provided him an outlet to supply his own needs at reduced cost.

Once he gained access to his own supply, it occurred to him that there must be other people in the same spot he was in. Then he put two and two together and looked at his father's grocery store through new eyes. Much as with silicon for computers, or radio signals that became pagers that became cell phones, by appraising the situation from puzzle mind instead of problem mind, he was able to reorder what already existed into a very creative little business. Amazing, to say the least. His penchant for puzzles was the catalyst that helped an entire industry get off the ground!

In Chapter 2, we also talked about the difference between being "directionally correct" and "perfectionally correct." Irwin did not come anywhere close to being perfect in anything, from his vision, to his ideas and plans, to his execution. He just had an intention (access to natural foods at a lower cost), which he was able to satisfy through a couple of small, incremental steps. As he did, he had the pleasure of seeing his vision and his intention grow.

There's a lot more to this story. For now, though, let's stick with the fundamental proposition: by framing his "problem" as a "puzzle" with a "solution" on the other side, this 19-year-old kid was able to become a leader in a brand-new industry. In the process, he met with the people who later started Celestial Seasonings Tea Company, Arrowhead Mills, and many other successful enterprises. His little idea of selling natural products on a rack in his father's store led to a natural foods distribution company that helped countless other small guys with cool ideas to expand.

"WHAT DO YOU MEAN I CAN'T GO HOME?"

You remember our friend Mitchell from the Introduction? He's the guy who was paralyzed in a plane crash four years after recovering from the burns he received over 65 percent of his body in a motorcycle crash. Must be some kind of cat! Mitchell was hospitalized for months at a specialty care facility treating people with spinal cord injuries, where he encountered a lot of what could be perceived as problems.

Rehabilitation is lengthy and grueling, to say the least. What with all the time he had spent in and out of hospitals recovering from his nearly fatal motorcycle accident and now paralysis, Mitchell was both eager to go home and increasingly savvy in the ways of hospitals. He had been undergoing rehabilitation for months when he finally decided that home was where he needed to be. He had a chat with his rehab specialist, Beverly, and informed her that he would be going home in a week. Beverly checked the chart and commented that she didn't see any notation to that effect and that surely the physician in charge would need to agree.

That promptly presented Mitchell with another opportunity to clarify his intention, take advantage of his ability to control what he could, and put in place an influence strategy for the rest. The first thing he had to do was enlist Beverly in the effort. That didn't prove too difficult given the relationship they had developed.

The next workaround challenge would be the physician in charge. Every Monday, Mitchell and his rehab team would meet in a conference room to discuss his progress, air any issues they were facing, and decide on the next course of rehabilitation treatment. The physician in charge always took the seat at the head of the table, and everyone else clustered around the leader.

Monday came, and Mitchell arrived in his wheelchair much earlier than anyone else. He rearranged the chairs, moving the one at the head of the table to a position along the side, and placed himself and his wheelchair in the leadership spot. When people began arriving, Mitchell thanked them for coming as usual and invited them to take a seat. The chief physician arrived and appeared taken aback to see his customary spot occupied. Mitchell smiled, thanked him for coming, and asked him to take any open seat.

Once everyone was in place, Mitchell began by informing the group that he would be running the meeting today. He then delivered his somewhat startling announcement: "I will be going home next week. Let me thank you for all your invaluable assistance in my recovery and rehabilitation. Any questions?"

The physician responded that he didn't think Mitchell was ready to go home and began to poll all the specialists in the room for their opinions on his readiness. At that point, thanks to a combination of Mitchell's intention and the preparation he had done with his rehab supervisor, Beverly reframed the question for the team: "Mitchell is not asking if he is ready; he is telling us he is leaving. The real question for us becomes, 'What do we need to do in order to assure that he is ready to go home next week?'"

Need I add that Mitchell went home? He returned a year later for some additional rehabilitation, having learned that there were still things he needed to learn. Did he regret leaving early? Not in the slightest! And the way he got out was by simply reframing the problem from why he couldn't leave into what would be necessary to make it possible. Sometimes—in fact, just about all the time—the only real issue is how you define the issue.

THE PRICE OF WALNUTS

As you may assume, my friend Irwin had many opportunities to apply his approach to problem solving as he built Tree of Life from a corner store into a leading distributor of natural foods. His preference for puzzles over problems led to creative solution after creative solution. Here's another he shared with me a few years into the distribution business:

> Years ago, when I used to do a lot of my own bulk buying of nuts and fruit commodities, shelled walnuts were getting really tight, and we did not have a good supply lined up for the year. I was training Sam, an experienced employee, to do our buying. He came in to see me late in the afternoon one day and told me he could not find any walnuts at a good price. This was the kind of challenge that I liked.
>
> Since I always worked late and typically bought all my nuts out of California, I got out a *Thomas Grocery Register* and started looking up nut suppliers from around the country, but mainly in California. I started making a few calls. Within two or three hours, I had tracked down a walnut supplier who had about a half of a truckload of walnuts left. I managed to buy his whole supply of walnuts, which was more than we would normally use, but the price was too good to refuse, and I knew I could easily sell them.
>
> In this instance, Sam had been out in the market trying to buy and wound up losing his own perception as he talked to everyone about how bad the crop was and how tight the market was. In that situation and that kind of business, I always was pretty good at maintaining a pretty factual and clear perception, and that gave me the ability

to look at things much differently from my employees and often reframe things in company meetings in order to shift the energy and feeling in the company into a different direction.

It was the very nature of someone's coming to me with a problem that got me excited and challenged to have fun with finding the solution. I think we both know, perception has a lot to do with how we move forward in our lives. Perception in this case did not include the word *problem*; it was more like a game that I liked to play.

THE LAST THING A FISH NOTICES IS WATER

At the risk of dating myself, I'm rolling the clock back a few decades with this next example. Personal computing was just coming about, and a couple of companies had missed the mark badly. For instance, take the now hilarious statement by Ken Olsen, founder and CEO of Digital Equipment Corporation, in 1977: "There is no reason for any individual to have a computer in his home."

Oops.

I had an early "portable" computer, alternately referred to as a "luggable" or simply "the sewing machine." It was at the outset of my consulting career helping organizations figure out what they needed to do in order to execute their strategies more efficiently, if not more effectively. One of the major computer manufacturers got wind of the work my firm was doing in aerospace and how our approach helped shorten development time lines while still ensuring superb quality. We were invited to the company's research facility, where internal engineers were working on developing a laptop computer.

When we arrived on the scene, we discovered that they did, in fact, have a prototype laptop already in existence. The only problem was the size of lap that you would need in order to use the monster—it weighed in at 34 pounds! As we snooped around the labs, we found an entire storeroom stuffed with competitors' computers, many of the luggable variety. Each had been cataloged relative to its technical specs, capabilities, and perceived shortcomings. That storeroom was our first clue as to what the issue might be.

Our engineer guides then took us to the workbench where the members of the engineering team went about designing their laptop. Each engineer sat in front of a workstation with a huge computer screen. Each screen was divided into quarters, and each quadrant was the size of a normal monitor. Each quadrant displayed data and design ideas from entirely different databases, each of which was powered by an entirely separate computer!

Can you see the issue we began to see? Here we had an engineering team designing a laptop using tools and technologies that only the most sophisticated technology companies could access. Whenever the engineers started putting their gear together with a combination of design specs and technical specs, they kept running out of room. The machine they were designing was just too small.

Sure, the world had yet to develop much in the way of today's miniaturization capabilities; however, that wasn't the real problem. The real problem was that the engineers were trying to design something that would work for what they thought were important computing needs, not what the traveling businessperson might need. No sooner did they come up with a prototype than they discovered just one more feature they couldn't live without.

We went back to our management sponsor and pointed out what we had learned. The response? Well, suffice it to say that the managers didn't see what we saw, most likely because they swam in the same ocean as the engineering team.

There's an old Zen saying that the last thing a fish ever notices is water. Kind of obvious, really: if you live in water your entire life, how would you ever notice unless it dried up? The problem was that both management and the design team were comfortably ensconced in their everyday milieu while trying to design a computer for someone who would never come close to approximating the computing environment that the team found commonplace.

Workaround: Reframe the Problem

We took the design team back to the storage room and asked each member to grab one of the "luggables" from the shelf. We then sent them on a two-week road trip, each flying alone around the country, staying at different hotels, and working from odd locations. Part of the assignment was to design the next-generation laptop using the luggable instead of the comfortably complex systems back at the lab.

When they got back to the lab two weeks later, they all had stories to tell about challenges they had faced. Would you be surprised to learn that the team quickly discovered numerous "requirements" that they could live without while on the road? That led to the next prototype's coming in at 17 pounds. Now, that is not exactly light, but compared with the 34-pound-monster predecessor, it was featherweight.

By taking the members of the engineering team out of their normal routine and having them reframe the problem via direct experience, we were able to work around their natural tendency to keep looking for new features, all of which were pretty easy to add in the accommodating confines of a superbly equipped lab. As soon as they began to live and work in an environment approximating that of their eventual users, they quickly hit upon features that weren't so necessary.

WASTE NOT, WANT NOT

Have you ever purchased fresh soup at a grocery store? Ever wonder how it is that grocery stores decided that offering their own soup and other prepared foods was a good thing? Sure, it all seems so convenient now that thousands of establishments sell these kinds of foods. However, the idea didn't start with customer service in mind! It really stems from a common problem all grocery stores face, something they call "shrink."

Here I have one more story to share about my friend Irwin. He eventually sold Tree of Life and decided to open a small grocery store in Santa Barbara, California, called Lazy Acres. True to form, Lazy Acres featured natural and organic products and quickly became a destination shop for consumers from miles around. As a grocery store owner now, Irwin was faced with another set of problems/puzzles: waste.

Grocery stores throw away otherwise fine produce every day on account of cosmetic damage. Many shoppers refuse to buy fruits or vegetables that have been bruised or that bear some other kind of natural "imperfection." Produce can also suffer cosmetic effects from causes such as light exposure and the natural gas emitted by ripening fruit, which accelerates ripening. In the trade, this situation is often referred to as "shrink," and it can amount to 5 percent of a store's produce.

Everyone in the grocery business is concerned about the shrink "problem," and people have taken a wide variety of measures to try to lessen or prevent it. At Lazy Acres, wasted product, or shrinkage, was running at a rate of around 320 pounds a day, or roughly $5,000 a week! How's that for a workaround challenge worth puzzling over? Most attempts to address the situation usually end up proving costly, such as having employees weigh and measure your purchase for you right in the produce department or using specialty packaging and display units.

Here's how Irwin arrived at the creative workaround for Lazy Acres: First, he had all those veggies to deal with. Then he noticed that the deli and meat departments were producing their own waste, primarily in the form of bones from roasts, turkeys, and other meats. One day, the shrinkage puzzle merged with his love of cooking, and he discovered a natural workaround for all that waste—soup! No one cares if the carrots are bruised in soup, and bones are a large part of the flavoring.

By approaching the shrink "problem" as a "puzzle," Irwin was able to not only "solve" the problem and "prevent" it from ever again being perceived as a problem but also turn shrink into a profitable source of value for his customers. Soup! By reframing shrinkage as a puzzle rather than a problem, Irwin succeeded in generating profits from something that otherwise would have been a loss. Using the cosmetically unappealing vegetables for soup, he transformed soup into the most profitable item in the store.

WORKAROUND QUESTIONS

When you're confronted with challenging situations—problems, as the world would call them; puzzles, as Irwin prefers—the most important factor is what you are telling yourself about the situation. If you have challenges dealing with other people, other departments, or company practices, your ability to work with them successfully will be determined in large measure by how you think about them. Anything you label as difficult will be difficult; anything you call a problem will be problematic. Instead, reframe the challenge or problem into a solution waiting to be found. Much as with opening a jigsaw puzzle box, you will be presented with lots of pieces. As an aid, the box comes with a picture on it. Your task when dealing with the puzzles of life is to build your own picture.

If you need to get someone on your side, working with you rather than against you, start by considering what the other party is charged with doing in his or her job, and then begin imagining how that person can win by helping you. Mitchell succeeded in gaining early discharge from the hospital by pointing the discussion toward what the specialists could do to help him solve the puzzle of going home, rather than being stuck with the problem that they thought he had—needing more hospital-centered treatment. Here are a few questions that may be helpful:

1. What is the problem you are facing?

2. How is it impacting you?

3. Who else is impacted?

4. What would it look like if the problem (puzzle) were solved?

5. How would you be impacted by a successful outcome?

6. How would the other people or groups be impacted by a successful outcome?

7. What can you do on your own to move forward?

8. How can you invite someone to "play" or help with the solution instead of being mired in the problem? (People much prefer to be seen as someone who can help rather than someone who is in the way.)

5

Communication and Action

All business problems are communications problems. In my years working as a business consultant and educational psychologist, I have seen conflicts of all kinds play out between internal units, between supervisor and subordinate, between customer and supplier, between alliance partners, and between business entities and regulators. As varied as they may be, they all have one factor in common: they started as communication issues.

Courses in effective communications all make attempts at improving this apparently difficult thing to do—to communicate. Each of us has probably heard the drill: listen first, speak second; paraphrase before adding your own thoughts; don't interrupt. And precious little of this makes any apparent difference.

As an educational psychologist, I spent considerable time early in my career wondering about the source of conflict and miscommunication. Whether in one-to-one counseling situations, working with groups, or trying to build teams, I have seen the communication issue rise over and over again. I must admit that before I really understood the problem, I spent a lot of time trying to teach people all the various active-listening skills from unconditional positive regard to how to paraphrase and seek mutual understanding.

I don't think the problem lies in various listening skills. However, before going further into the source of common communication issues, I want to underscore that effective listening skills are an important part of the solution. It has been my experience that people clearly don't know how to listen very well. Part of the listening problem stems from how much emphasis we place on the ability to make a case, to advocate a point of view, to argue for a position. If we have been trained in the art of making a strong case for our point of view, many of us therefore might have learned to listen not so much to understand the other as to be able to offer a counterargument.

There is an old Buddhist saying that asks: "Are you listening, or just preparing to speak?" There is a big difference between conversing with someone who is listening to understand and conversing with someone who is listening to argue. I'm sure you have experienced the contrast! We have all had to face people who listen solely for the purpose of countering whatever we have to say, even without having a point of their own to offer. For these folks, the main purpose of conversation doesn't touch on having a good debate ("my point is stronger and more well-thought-out than yours"); it is more about discrediting the other person, finding holes in the other's logic, or otherwise appearing superior through the ability to find fault.

Have you ever been on the wrong end of a conversation with someone who has been through one of those effective-listening courses? In this instance, I am not referring to someone who is seeking to listen and to paraphrase before responding; rather, I mean the person who has mastered the art of what I call "malicious listening." The malicious listener is skilled at listening with a not-so-hidden motive. This person listens to prove you wrong and uses your own words to make his or her case. This type can quote you ("you said . . .") and quickly follow with a retort, rejoinder, or snide comment about how wrong you are.

An often efficient workaround for malicious listeners is to thank them for listening so attentively and then ask if they could add a few more thoughts on the implications of what you just said. Asking someone what the underlying meaning might be rather than the actual words used generally has a way of stopping the malicious listener cold.

WHAT YOU HEARD IS NOT WHAT I MEANT

Much as with the proverbial iceberg, the words we say frequently represent only a small percentage of what's below the surface. If you have acquired the listening skill to repeat what was said, you may be able to get the words right and still miss the important part of the message. Here's an example of how things can go awry even though the words repeated seem to match the words originally spoken:

A team was meeting to try to find a solution to a problem it had encountered in working with another group. Joe had been contributing to the brainstorming of options, and Susan was feeling a bit threatened about the direction things were going. Joe realized that the purpose of brainstorming is not to arrive at a perfect solution but is instead to develop possible options for consideration. In fact, Joe recognized that some of his ideas held only a kernel of possibility, but he also knew that getting those kernels out is part of the process.

Susan had heard all she wanted to hear and, instead of contributing to the brainstorming, turned her attention to what she called "Joe's half-baked ideas." Not sure where she was going with this comment, Joe asked if she could elaborate. That was just the opening Susan was hoping for, and she started to tear into him, citing exactly what he had said, word for word. Joe was in an awkward spot: she was accurately quoting him but missing his point. He could start to argue, telling her she was missing the point, and he could even challenge her to come up with something better—all of which could easily lead to an even more disagreeable interaction.

Instead, Joe calmly acknowledged that those were the words he had used and the ideas he was generating. Knowing that the words were accurate but the meaning was missed, Joe said, "Thanks for listening so closely to me. What strikes you as my underlying purpose in sharing these kernels of an idea?"

The purpose of this question was to change the nature of the discussion. People can get hung up on the precision of what was said and, in so doing, miss the purpose of what was said. Often, that has a lot more to do with how the listener interprets statements than with the actual words that were used. By turning the conversation away from the precise words and over to the underlying purpose or impact, you can frequently work around the apparent disagreement and get moving in a more fruitful direction.

Susan scolded Joe, claiming that she heard him saying she was doing a crummy job. Joe responded: "Wow, I hadn't thought about it that way before. I'm so sorry you felt attacked. What I was really trying to do was imagine ways we could all do an even better job. Are there ways you could imagine our group doing even better?" It took a couple more attempts, but eventually the conversation turned away from perceived attacks and toward a more productive discussion of improvement opportunities.

THE ROOTS OF COMMUNICATION

We have all encountered communications problems from time to time; in fact, we have all probably been the source of the problem for someone else. Regardless of your experience, there is a certain kind of communication challenge that you should be particularly aware of. What follows is an illustration of this problem, laid out in the form of a word game. This word game starts with my assertion that the majority of people don't know what the word *communication* really means. Now, of course you know what the word means in one sense, but my experience suggests that most people don't really know the purpose underlying the word. So, here goes:

Communication

Let's pretend that the word *communication* is actually made up of several words and that our job is to ferret them out, put them together, and then discover what the word actually means. Starting with the letter *c*, what is the first, little tiny word you can find inside the word *communication*? How about *co*? What does *co* mean? "Together," "with," and "part of" all come to mind. These preliminary definitions put us on the trail to meaning. Clearly, communication has something to do with being together.

How about the first two-syllable word? Starting again with the letter *c*, we come up with *commun*. What does *commun* suggest? Again, "together" and "part of." You can see it in words such as *community* and, well, *commune*. More togetherness.

Does *commun* look like another ordinary word, just slightly misspelled? How about changing the *u* to an *o*? That leaves us with:

Common

The suggestion here is that communication has something to with togetherness and "in common." Now take the last six letters in the word—*cation*. Does that look like another familiar word, with the letters slightly out of order? How about reversing the *c* and the *a*? That leaves us with:

Action

In fact, just about any word in English, or in French, or Spanish, or Italian, that ends in *ion, tion,* or *ation* means "requires action." More on that later.

Put those two together, and what do you get?

Common Action

or

Commun i cation

With this little word game in mind, we then have the word *communication* meaning something about acting together or acting in common. The keys are "action" and "in common."

So, if the purpose of communication is "common action," then what does that mean? My suggestion is that the only time we ever bother "communicating" with another person is when we want something from that person—it could be approval, cooperation, support, encouragement, or just plain companionship. What happens when we don't want or need anything from the other person? Usually, we don't bother saying anything at all!

If we are looking to "act in common" with another person, what do we *both* need to know before that can happen? If you are looking for approval, support, or cooperation, a good follow-up line of inquiry may be: approval, support, or cooperation in service to what? If we are going to act together, we probably need to know something about what we are acting together for—some sense of direction or purpose.

Taking this one step further, then, we have the word *communication* looking something like this:

Common Action

(acting in common)

Toward

(a commonly held)

Purpose
Outcome
Goal
Objective
Result

Now, think back to the last time you had a "miscommunication" at home or at work, and I'll bet you can confirm that you and the other person (or team) had differing versions of the purpose, outcome, or goal. If this rings even slightly true, then I'll also bet that your actual conversation was more about the action (who is going to do what) and less about the purpose, outcome, or goal.

The problem, of course, is that if the two parties involved don't take the time to make certain that they are on the same page in terms of overall purpose and outcome, each is likely to start taking actions toward something slightly different, if not immensely different. And then what happens when it becomes evident that one party failed to meet the other party's criteria of a "good outcome"? One of them may feel that the other person "screwed up." Or didn't understand. Or didn't explain it well. Or didn't try hard enough. Or. Or. Or.

From there, it can become comical, perhaps even pathetic. How often have you experienced some kind of miscommunication or failed outcome and then found everyone focused on the "action" part of the equation? "Tell me again what you heard you were supposed to do?" "Tell me again what you did." "Let's review the action plan one more time."

The assumption in these kinds of "review" conversations is that someone dropped the ball at the action level. "Do it again, harder" becomes the mantra of improvement. And maybe it is just a question of doing it again. By the same token, though, doing it again could evoke Einstein's definition of insanity as doing the same thing over and over and expecting a different result.

It is probably painfully obvious by now where we are heading with this. There are times when reviewing the action plan or action sequence makes sense; however, before going over the actions taken or not taken, the first order of review should be to go over the intended purpose and outcome, to make certain that everyone was on the same page to begin with. If the two parties have different versions of a good outcome right from the get-go, you can pretty much predict disaster, or at least disappointment, downstream.

WORKAROUNDS FOR BETTER COMMUNICATION

Start any "communication" with a discussion about your individual perceptions of the intended purpose, outcome, and goal. Make certain that both of you can explain the desired outcome in terms that the other can both repeat and visualize:

- What do you imagine the outcome looking like?

- What will be produced?

- What will it be able to do?

- Why would we want that?

These are some of the kinds of questions that will help both of you verify that you are on the same page in regard to outcomes and general direction.

Then, spend some time on action steps and responsibilities:

- Who will be response-able for doing what?

- What are the deliverables that each person will be producing? What are the time lines or milestones?

- What are the consequences of missing a time line or milestone for other team members?

- What should we do if one or the other is in danger of missing a milestone or actually misses one?

- What impact will missing a milestone have on the desired outcome?

- What should we do if one of us needs help?

There are hundreds of questions you can conceivably ask, and the intent here is not to provide a definitive list. Rather, it is to demonstrate the value of clarifying the outcome as well as the actions required to produce the outcome.

Communication, then, is the process of defining a commonly held purpose, outcome, or goal along with a commonly agreed-upon set of actions to get there.

WITHOUT COMMUNICATION, THERE IS CONFLICT

Leaving the corporate world for a moment, let's check in with a couple who are planning for their "relaxing" vacation in Hawaii.

HIM: "I sure could use some time to unwind and just relax."

HER: "Me too. Hawaii would be great."

HIM: "Hawaii. What a great idea. Warm, sunny, relaxing."

HER: "Perfect. Beaches, pools, scenic vistas. Just perfect."

HIM. "All right! Hawaii it is."

HER: "I can't wait."

Now let us skip ahead to the day before they leave. Watch them pack for the trip (taking action).

HIM: "Golf clubs, tennis rackets, snorkel gear, hiking boots."

HER: "Suntan lotion, collection of books, swimsuits."

Do you see the potential for conflict? I have certainly seen it play out in real life.

"But I thought you agreed this would be a relaxing trip—just time to unwind and let go?"

His version? Unwind equals run around, hit balls, exercise.

Her version? Unwind equals downtime, soak up some rays, enjoy doing nothing at the beach.

The mere fact that you can agree with someone on the "purpose" doesn't mean you actually have the same thing in mind. In this example, the difference between sports equipment and suntanning gear should point to possible conflicts once both people arrive in Hawaii. Similarly, in Chapter 3 we observed misaligned leaders who could all articulate the same vision statement but who nevertheless produced 18 answers to the question about their company's top three goals.

Before assuming every member of your team is on the same page, spend some time discussing the purpose to be achieved and what the team imagines it will look like when you get there. The more detail, the better. Then you can each get going on the "action" side of "common." If this trouble area seems even remotely familiar, just envision how hard it can be to keep the "communication" in the right direction as you roll down three layers in an organization, or even as a project moves along through different departments!

WORKAROUND QUESTIONS

Here are a few core questions to consider that can have the effect of warding off problems before they have a chance to manifest:

1. What goals or objectives are we shooting for?

2. What will it look like when we get there?

3. What will we have to be good at to get there?

4. What projects will we have to deliver to get there?

5. Who has what roles, rights, and responsibilities along the way?

6. What action steps will be taken? Who will take them?

7. How will we report our progress along the way?

6

Accountability and Response-Ability

The words in this chapter's title can either strike fear in the heart or liberate the soul. I suggest that we work on liberation. All too often, accountability and responsibility equate to the general notion of blame or fault. "Who's responsible for this?" is a question sure to instill fear in most people at any given time. Hearing the words "We're holding you accountable" can be equally terrifying.

Can you conceive of someone asking, "Who's responsible for this great success?" with the same vigor with which he or she may ask, "Who's responsible for this great mess?" Not too readily, would be my guess. Same thing goes for "We're holding you accountable for these great numbers" versus "We're holding you accountable for these delays."

Given that it's apparently human nature to look to blame someone else when things go badly, or to assume credit when things go well, it's not surprising that many people seem to duck responsibility and accountability. I am firmly of the mind that accountability and responsibility are absolute keys to power and the ability to create more of what you want in life. No matter the circumstance or situation in which you may be plopped, there will always be choices you can make that can help you move forward. When you're confronting difficult work situations, whether in the form of broken processes, misaligned teams, uncooperative coworkers, or unclear communications, workarounds can be found, but only if you are first willing to seek them out and then willing to take the actions necessary.

While part of the strategy is influencing someone else to think or act differently, if we simply wait for someone else to figure it out and do the right thing, we may make little progress. Make no mistake: if the situation were going to improve because of someone else's acting independently, it would already have happened. So, if you're the one who notices, then you're the one who is going to have to take the first steps to get something going. This is where response-ability and accountability enter the picture.

As you will see, accountability can function as a kind of North Star, an internal guidepost that keeps you on track by dint of one simple internal choice: the willingness to own the outcome and everything it takes to get there. If you commit to owning the outcome, you will then be able to exercise your response-ability through the control and influence choices we have been discussing all along. Asking yourself those two questions about what you can do that would make a difference is nothing more than making an assessment of the situation and figuring out ways in which you can act on it.

As noted in the first chapter, any workaround recipe requires the same three basic ingredients before anything can change or improve:

1. **Intention:** your focus and commitment to making a needed change

2. **Accountability:** your willingness to own the outcome

3. **Response-ability:** your choice to control and influence what you can

Combine a clear intention with a rational assessment of your ability to respond, and you may well be on your way to some very successful outcomes.

OWN IT ALL

It's easy for most of us to own the good stuff—our accomplishments and successes—even if we are suitably modest in our willingness to claim credit. However, owning it all, including what works, what doesn't work, and even what completely falls flat, could be the most powerful of all intentions. Whether it's getting to Louisville when there are no flights or overcoming incredible adversity as Mitchell has done, there is limitless power in not only clarifying your intention but also then owning everything it will take to get there. If you were to read Mitchell's life story, you would notice his constant focus on his response-ability for dealing with his circumstances. He doesn't spend time blaming himself or anyone else. Instead, he is intent on owning the kind of life he would like to create and doing what he can despite the many physical challenges.

That old saw from Chapter 1 bears repeating: 99 percent is a bitch, 100 percent is a breeze. What this is really saying is that you need to commit to your outcomes completely. Even a hint of hesitation or doubt, if allowed to persist, will sink your ship. Without 100 percent commitment, David might still be in LAX or Mitchell might have remained languishing in a hospital rehab unit for months on end.

The world is full of people who are willing to do "just so much." These are the 99 percent people. Then there are the 100 percent folks, those who are focused and committed to the outcome, the "whatever it takes" people. It's kind of like being 99 percent committed to jumping across the chasm—99 percent of the way is still going to set you up for a long fall.

The willingness to own it all—the outcome, the choices you will have to make, and the experience you will have to go through—empowers you to make life work well, to overcome hurdles and roadblocks, and to create workarounds that work. At the center of any situation you face, whether it is going smoothly or running aground, you will inevitably have a choice about how you respond. If nothing else, you always have some control over your responses. You may not have as many choices as you would like, but however limited the field of options may seem, you do get to choose. That's good as far as it goes, but what happens when the rest of the team is singing from a different song sheet? In particular, what if the entire culture is one of fear and blame?

LIVING IN A CULTURE OF FEAR AND BLAME

When problems occur in Japanese companies and American companies, conventional wisdom suggests you can differentiate between the two cultures quickly. The American company will spend valuable time and resources finding out how to affix blame. The Japanese company will spend time and resources trying to figure out how to fix the problem. At this writing, we have an immediate opportunity to see if this adage proves true regarding the Toyota fiasco over braking and acceleration problems. The American press is all over the situation with story after story pointing fingers at those to blame.

In one sense, figuring out where blame lies seems like a natural thing to do. After all, the problem didn't create itself now, did it? Surely someone created it. So, let's find that someone and . . . and what? Fix that person's wagon? Fix the problem? Or simply administer punishment? Over the past few years, corporations have increasingly adopted accountability as the new mantra to redress problems. If you work in an environment where people are more accustomed to the blame side of accountability and responsibility, though, you probably won't see many people rushing to the front of the line when problems crop up, at least not to accept responsibility.

In fact, in the more toxic blame-oriented cultures, people may tend to rush to the front of the line to point fingers. Or, perhaps equally destructively, they may retreat further into the woodwork, ducking visibility, while quietly assembling documentation to show that the problem lies elsewhere. So, if you've got a problem to overcome, something that is impeding your ability to get something done, do you need more people blaming one another? Do you need more people you can blame? Do you need more people blaming you?

But the Other Guy Did It. No, Really.

Imagine you are part of a team working on a complex, highly technical project that requires significant contributions from and interactions with several other teams in order to produce the intended outcome. What do you do when your part of the project is impacted by work that another person or team performs? What if you can't start until that other piece is done? What if the person or team is late, and you get blasted by senior management because you're late and you're the one who is visible? Or what if you're working on a joint project with another company, and the late deliverable is coming from that company?

Sound familiar? I have seen this kind of situation play out time and time again in a wide range of industries, including technology, health care, power generation, aerospace, pharmaceuticals, and telecommunications, to name but a few. So, what do you do when the other guy is late? One response is to start waving the red flag and sending out CYA memos to those who will notice, making certain that it is clear where the blame lies. That may strike you as a reasonable path, but stop and think: what kind of impact do you expect that to have long term? How would you expect the other person, team, or company to respond downstream?

Of course, you could always go to these individuals, teams, or companies and start reading them the riot act. Better yet, you could escalate to someone higher up the food chain, being sure to emphasize the other guy's faults and how they are making life difficult for you. Once again, neither approach figures to produce surefire success or increased cooperation in the future.

Returning to our imaginary technical project, what can you do now? Rather than firing up the blame machine and going on the offensive, how about going to members of the other team and asking a couple of questions? The first step would be to ask if there is something you and your team could contribute to help them produce what you need. A companion question would be to ask if there is anything you or your team may be doing that makes it difficult for them to execute. Third, and even more powerful, would be to invite the other team to envision scenarios in which the whole situation were to improve and ask, "What would you suggest that we do differently or more creatively?" You may be impressed by how much you can learn, and correct, just by posing these three questions. Being asked for their help is a heck of a lot more appealing to people than being asked to accept blame for the problem *you* are experiencing. Yes, they may be contributing to the challenge, but giving them an opportunity to contribute is way more attractive than giving them the opportunity to be blamed.

Example: Satco

Here's an instructive example of how a company discovered that it had become its own worst enemy. The managers started out thinking they had to devise a workaround strategy for a difficult supplier. What they learned instead was that they had to work around their own internal processes, which were making it difficult for the supplier to perform. As you will see, they crafted a creative but simple influence strategy to solve a complex, challenging problem.

Relayco had been supplying a critical part to Satco for use in satellites the company was building for the U.S. government. A long string of contentious technical and quality issues coupled with delivery delays led Relayco to announce that it would exit the business altogether. This put Satco in a dire situation as it tried to get the remaining parts needed to complete the satellite.

Satco first went on the attack, threatening litigation and the involvement of the government to force the supplier into compliance. Relayco remained resolute in its decision to close this unprofitable line. Recognizing that they could neither control the situation nor intimidate Relayco into performing, the managers at Satco made a switch in tactics. Employing some of what they had learned from me on workaround strategies, they decided to take the response-able approach and seek ways to influence the other side.

Abandoning the clearly useless approach of blame and intimidation, Satco managers started asking questions about what it would take to get the needed parts. They asked Relayco to identify any issues or roadblocks that were preventing it from performing. This request opened the floodgates of useful information. The first thing Satco managers learned was that someone on their own contracting team had taken the unprecedented step of demanding a number of test cycles that was three times the industry standard. That level of vigorous testing was bound to result in a lower yield of parts that could pass muster. Satco immediately offered to reduce the test cycles back to the industry standard.

Even lowering the testing cycles would improve yield by only 10 percent, though. So, Satco pressed on, asking what else was in the way, and learned of an onerous term that had been slipped into the agreement by someone in procurement. This term allowed Relayco to rework any defective part discovered at the Relayco site but required scrapping a defective part if it was discovered at the Satco facility. Recognizing the insanity of that term, Satco immediately rescinded it. Relayco's attitude began to change noticeably, and 22 additional parts were back on the line.

They then discovered one more incomprehensible term that procurement had inserted, increasing the tolerance requirements to double that of the industry standard. Given that the industry was about satellite performance and this was a satellite being built, no one could understand the need for that increased tolerance demand, and it, too, was retired. If the performance standard is double the norm, and testing cycles are triple, it's not hard to compute why Relayco was having so much difficulty.

Having changed its influence strategy from that of blame and issuing threats to one of shared response-ability, Satco was able to fulfill the contract and also create a friend where before it had an unhappy supplier. With these changes in hand, Relayco did not close its doors as it had intended and had committed to its investors. Satco also used the lessons learned with Relayco to assess other contracts under which performance was suboptimal. In many of them, Satco discovered that rather than needing to work around difficult suppliers, it really needed to work around its own contracting processes.

I hope you can see that by dropping the blame and fear game, it is possible to reach powerful and effective outcomes. Once again, the workaround is a combination of intention (getting useful parts) and control (fixing what you can on your own) and then seeking to influence the other to collaborate on the solution.

In this particular instance, the Satco manager chose to circumvent his company's norm of issuing threats through a combination of the legal department and senior vice presidents and went directly to the management of the supplier. He focused on fixing the problem, not affixing blame; his attitude was one of partnering and shared response-ability.

Take note that while some workarounds can appear to slow down the process, they can actually speed things up. In this case, the outcome speaks for itself.

Even if your company runs on the fear and blame version of accountability, you don't have to play along. By forthrightly adopting a mind-set of owning the outcome (accountability) and seeking creative choices (response-ability), you can begin to make big differences in how problems are resolved and results produced. Approaching people and situations that require workarounds can be done from the fear and blame perspective, but those workarounds are usually not sustainable. Few people are going to be interested in finding yet another opportunity to be blamed.

If, instead, you start with the perspective that there are solutions available and that the other guy would like to share in the improvement, you will soon unveil powerful influence choices. As odd and perhaps risky as it may seem, owning the outcome and asking the other person for input on what you could do differently creates two distinct improvement opportunities: you may learn something that you can do that you had not previously seen, and you also model the premise that finding solutions beats the heck out of finding people to blame. This simple shift has the effect of producing partners where previously you might have had adversaries.

WORKAROUND QUESTIONS

While there are endless situations that you can improve by adopting this "own the outcome" mind-set, you can loosely group most workarounds into two basic categories: those in which you will need to do something different and those in which someone else will need to do something different. One of the hardest things to determine right up front is which category is going to be in play.

Once you have asked yourself the basic starting question— "What can I do that will make a difference?"—and asked the other party if there's anything else you can do, you can then turn the question toward what the other party could conceive of doing to make the situation even better. The questions that follow may be helpful in enlisting the other party's support in coming up with creative solutions:

1. Are there improvements you could imagine to this process or outcome?

2. What could we do together that would make a difference?

3. Is there any support you need from me?

4. Are there improvements you could imagine from another group or department?

5. Who would have to be on board to make these changes?

6. How could we influence them?

7

Breakdowns
Between Silos

A recurrent challenge confronting organizations large and
small is that of silo behavior. We broached this subject in
Chapter 3 when talking about misaligned leadership.

Breakdowns between silos can occur among internal groups,
departments, or business units as well as among external partners,
subcontractors, or teammates on joint development projects.

Often, internal conflicts breed between groups because the
groups have slightly different missions. If you are on the front
lines, whether in manufacturing, interacting with customers, or
managing suppliers, you are trying to get something across the
finish line. In order to get that airplane manufactured, get that
seminar delivered, or get that pharmaceutical released, you may
have to deal with any number of internal groups before you can
gain sign-off for the next step, much less for final delivery.

Hands down, compliance and risk management are critical to
the long-term success of any organization, and there are internal
groups within most organizations whose primary duty is to
ensure that people follow procedures. Just as certain, there are
times when compliance can become an end in itself rather than a

truly helpful process. Most people will recognize this state of control as part of the bureaucratic turf, but what happens when the compliance system starts to create problems of its own? And what happens when internal groups fail to talk to one another?

Let's briefly turn our sights again to the example in Chapter 2 of the state of California and the policy of requiring compliance with nonexistent regulations. Those controls were initially put there for a powerful and positive reason: to minimize waste and assure appropriate expenditure of public funds. With the passage of time, the controls had taken on a life and purpose of their own, so much so that they were actually generating waste themselves, while inhibiting the delivery of services they were meant to assure. The problem stemmed from a situation that unfortunately is probably all too prevalent in government as well as organizations large and small: different groups are marching to independent drummers who are apparently part of the same band.

In this example, the state had several silos operating at the same time, each unaware of the impact one was having on the others. The legislative branch issued new regulations from time to time. Agencies developed their own rules and regulations. Contracts put the rules and regulations into terms and conditions. Various audit and compliance-monitoring groups enforced the rules and regulations.

Seems innocent enough, even logical, doesn't it? The hitch was that no one on the legislative or regulatory side bothered to communicate with the contracts group when laws expired or regulations changed. This is an example of where the "stop" part of the start-stop-continue equation would have been useful.

The regulatory folks were pretty good at the "start" side—they let the contracts people know when new laws or regulations went into effect—just not so good at letting them know when something was no longer required. I'm only guessing here, but I'm willing to wager that job descriptions existed detailing what to pass on to contracts for inclusion, but nothing spelled out a job requirement to let contracts know when something should be deleted.

Similarly, once the contracts department included something, the document was thrown over the wall to the group that audited compliance. Auditors were narrowly tasked with ensuring that existing clauses were adhered to, not determining whether those clauses still mattered. The predictable net result was that the agency spent considerable time and resources monitoring requirements that no longer were relevant, and the actual nonprofit service groups were spinning their wheels instead of providing the services for which they were funded.

If you find yourself or your group in conflict with a part of the organization charged with following rules or procedures, it may be worthwhile to sit down with your counterparts to ensure that everyone is on the same page. Larry Senn's advice from the Introduction about "assuming innocence" offers a wise attitude to adopt when you start the conversation—the other group is most likely trying to ensure that something good takes place. Start by inquiring what that good outcome might be. From there, if you still have some differences, let your counterparts see what the situation looks like from your perspective or that of your customer, and solicit their suggestions on what might make the situation workable for both sides. The main concern, of course, is that both groups act in alignment toward the larger purpose or goal of the organization.

HOW DIFFERENT SILOS AFFECT EACH OTHER

Sometimes, the biggest improvement opportunities start right where you are. On many occasions, we have seen apparently large organizational issues virtually dissolve by simply asking three questions:

1. What needs improving around here and why?

2. What could you do that would make a difference that requires no one's permission other than your own? (Confine your answer to just your own job and what would make your job easier, more effective, or more productive.)

3. What could you do that would make a difference that requires permission, cooperation or approval? Whose? (Same context as above: what could you do that would make your job easier, more effective, or more productive but would also require someone else to go along?)

A while ago, my consulting firm had the opportunity to work with representatives of a hospital group in Florida. The client was experiencing performance issues ranging from patient satisfaction to cost management to physician engagement. We gathered roughly 450 managers, supervisors, and executives in a large theater-style conference facility. After an interactive session in which senior managers shared a few thoughts about where they were headed, we asked those 450 people in the room to take out their notebooks and work on the same three questions noted above, creating three separate lists.

Once people had completed their three lists, we asked them to seal list one and list three in a special envelope we provided them and to not refer to those lists until we got together again in a month's time. We further asked everyone in the room to spend the next month focusing their actions on list two: What could you do that would make a difference in your job that requires no one's permission other than your own?

When we reassembled a month later, the room was abuzz with people engaged in animated discussions. The energy level was much higher than it had been the previous month when we first convened. Can you guess what produced the buzz, the heightened energy in the room? Think back again to Chapter 2 and the effects associated with exercising or cleaning that refrigerator by accident. Same phenomenon here: people had spent the previous month doing simple things that were within their own control. Many had completed long-outstanding projects or had raised their level of performance to match their internal standards. By directing their attention to the fact that they could do something that would make a difference, they were able to take actions that made a difference.

That simple act of taking action (control) produced two powerful and energizing phenomena. First, getting something done released that stored-up psychic fat, providing more energy to do more things. Second, bringing their behavior into alignment with what they knew they could do to make a difference restored each of them to a higher sense of standards—"I'm the kind of person who takes responsibility and makes a difference"—which is probably what led these particular people to work in health care to begin with.

Getting stuff moving, making a difference, and doing so without needing anyone else to give them permission was empowering, exciting, and fulfilling. Hence, a roomful of excited people creating quite a buzz. We took a few comments from those present about the past month, all of which validated the general sense that things were moving. We then asked them to open that sealed envelope and to read list three.

Within minutes, the buzz was back in the room, only more so. We asked them what was up. With microphones placed around the room, we soon had individuals standing up and saying things like, "I had on my list that my job would improve if only Mike did xyz. Lo and behold, Mike did!" From there it was a short step to the discovery that Mike did whatever he did, not because it helped Claudia, but because it was on his list of things that would make his job better if only he were to do something himself. And he did.

They discovered as a group that a good 60 percent to 70 percent of the needed improvements could be had just by people's assuming individual responsibility for what they could do on their own and not waiting for someone else to take the initiative. What now remained were the much more strategic issues, the kind of improvements that did require cooperation, collaboration, and approval (influence). This little exercise enabled leadership to more quickly identify what was truly critical and allowed the native intelligence of the organization to come to the fore.

Senior leadership was then able to concentrate on its own role in setting direction, without spending so much time either blaming the workforce for being lazy, political, or otherwise ineffective or refereeing disputes between departments. The real kicker showed up over the next few months: many people found that it was much easier to influence others to cooperate, collaborate, or genially lend a hand when each took responsibility for his or her own part of the equation.

Too often it happens that attempting to influence others to change comes across as blame or criticism. This personal responsibility approach to control and influence can lead to much more fluid interactions and a shared sense of accomplishment. So, perhaps the workaround is yet again one that starts with you making the first move. That applies no matter what your station is in the organization, from the most senior to the most junior. We all have a role to play, so start at the center of the circle and exercise the control that truly is yours and yours alone.

THAT'S NOT *YOUR* JOB

We've all had brushes with the person who declines to do something under the age-old defense "that's not my job." How about the inverse of that one? Have you ever met up with someone who tried to stop you from doing something because "that's not your job"? That can be a really difficult roadblock, especially when you may need to work around someone who isn't engaged at the level required for you to proceed. Reasons abound for disengagement, ranging from it's not high enough on their priority list yet to they just don't want to get involved.

Here's a related example with a well-executed workaround:

The insurance company had several divisions, as well as multiple customer bases. There was the usual complement of large group, small group, and individual customers, along with different kinds of insurance programs that might be offered depending on customer type, location, and a couple other variables.

Health care reform was looming on the horizon, and although no one knew for sure where the legislation would finally land, it was pretty clear to all employees that the landscape would shift dramatically. The door was open to a wide set of products, depending on how the company wound up defining its customers and markets. Mindful of the insurer's history of moving slowly, hierarchically, and with considerable bureaucracy, people around the organization began positioning themselves for various possibilities in the new order.

A great way to build protection in an organization is to gather critical data and hoard it. As you might imagine, insurance companies have all kinds of deep information veins. However, the data were housed all over the organization. A new marketing director joined the company from outside the insurance industry and saw the potential for gathering all the data into one place. However, she was rebuffed by each of the product groups—the basic message being, "Butt out—that's not your job."

Rather than trying to persuade from within, which might have looked more like an internal raid than an offer of collaboration, she went to the outside and hired a well-respected data analyst. Once on board, the new analyst spent his first few months building relationships, asking a few questions, and sharing some of his insights and expertise along the way. By first seeking to understand the players and what was important to them, he was able to establish a strong influence position, which eventually resulted in various leaders asking him in to add even more value.

It didn't take long before he was able to call a summit meeting of all the groups to share some observations. As they began to see that each had similar issues, these groups also discovered opportunities that might arise from sharing data. The analyst was then able to turn their focus away from internal silo protection and back to the competitive world outside their own insurance company, helping them see new opportunities. At this writing, the organization is well on its way toward generating a powerful set of new, collaborative, cross-group offerings driven by its ability to share customer data and analyze the information against a variety of concerns and opportunities.

In the lexicon of workarounds, this collaboration process required thinking and acting on several fundamental levels. Let's review what happened in the context of how you might address an issue from several workaround perspectives.

1. **Environment response.** Just as the insurance company data analyst looked first to the competitive environment, are there external drivers that add weight to your argument that a workaround is needed?

2. **People do things for their reasons, not your reasons.** Even when people are behaving in a way that seems obstinate, they usually have what they consider to be a good reason. Try to find out what's motivating their behavior, and then look for ways you can actually help them accomplish what's important to them. By doing so, you stand to gain an ally or a partner rather than an impediment who has to be maneuvered.

3. **Control.** As always, look first to what you can do that requires no one's permission other than your own. In this instance, the data analyst found internal information sources that not only helped his cause but also provided useful information to those he was trying to influence.

4. **Influence.** Armed with valuable information and a sense of what was important to each of his key constituents, he was able to show people how it would be in their best interest to join the parade. What people do you need to have on board, and how might they benefit?

WHEN THE SILOS EXIST AT YOUR PARTNER

Dealing with silo behavior can be difficult enough when the silos are located in your own company. They aren't always, and you may find yourself faced with a different set of silo-related issues when your company needs to work together with your customer, your supplier, or your partner. Following is an example in which silo behavior in a partner company impacted the entire project.

The National Polar-Orbiting Operational Environmental Satellite System (NPOESS) was to be the United States' next-generation satellite system; it would monitor the earth's weather, atmosphere, oceans, land, and near-space environment. The estimated launch date for the first NPOESS satellite had slipped from an initial target of 2006 to 2013. Problems with sensor development were cited as the primary reason for delays and cost overruns. Partners Northrop Grumman and Raytheon were challenged to find solutions that would get the program back on track.

- **Roadblock:** By mid-December 2007, with the threat of cancellation hanging over the program, there were 3,032 open issues and a customer requirement that they be resolved within 60 days. Internal staffing coordinators within the subcontractor (sub) were also slowing things down as they sought to control engineers assigned to the program. Conflicts within internal groups (silos) at the sub meant that many matters were not being addressed. Each internal silo was clearly managing to its own set of objectives, few of which included improved performance of the NPOESS program.

- **Impact:** The continuing and escalating schedule delays resulted in cost overruns measured in excess of $1 million per day, which in turn produced a very unhappy customer threatening to quash the multibillion-dollar program.

- **Workaround:** The prime contractor (prime) needed to understand and accept the culture and capability of its sub. Realizing that the sub prided itself on its superior scientific capability and staffing excellence, representatives of the prime approached representatives of the sub with this line of reasoning: "With your technical and staffing expertise, surely you should be able to resolve these issues quickly." The pitch highlighted the sub's capabilities and included positive reinforcement that the prime had faith in the sub.

This approach leveraged the previously stated principle that people do things for their reasons, not your reasons. Rather than heap blame and abuse on the sub, by underscoring the sub's capabilities the prime encouraged the sub to overcome its own problems with silos through executive engagement. The prime and sub worked together to form a joint senior-level resolution process, effectively creating both decision and process workarounds. Issues were bucketed into 10 key categories, to be reviewed in twice-daily meetings between VPs from the two organizations. Each session identified open issues requiring senior-level involvement, what was needed to unstick the works, and what senior-level action would be taken.

- **Result:** With air cover provided by appropriate VPs, the teams managed to resolve 3,031 of the 3,032 open issues within the required time frame. The remaining issue required a bit more time to resolve but did wind up working out. Morale across the project rose considerably, particularly within the sub's culture. Engineers, managers, and contributors were able to see a direct impact from their involvement, and the sensor wound up working perfectly.

A DISCONNECT BETWEEN DEPARTMENTS

Sometimes breakdowns between silos can be so basic that they're actually humorous. Here is an example that will demonstrate how to get past such breakdowns. Data General was one of the first minicomputer firms to emerge in the late 1960s. A series of missteps in the 1980s led to a decline in market share, and the company was subsequently taken over by EMC in 1999.

Here's a classic case of silos failing to communicate. In the mid-1990s marketing created a clever program designed to drive inquiries to the sales group. The marketing program targeted the launch of a new computer with a unique ad campaign in which the computer was presented as looking for a job. Unfortunately, marketing neglected to clue sales in on the program, even though the sales phone number was listed in the materials.

Interested IT directors started spinning the dial to learn more about the position, and of course, sales had no idea what they were talking about. You can imagine the bizarre conversations that must have taken place! The impact is funny now, but I'm not so sure Sales was laughing at the time.

Workaround: Bridge the Gap

Rather than risk more embarrassing disconnects—and disconnects had been part of the chafing history between marketing and sales for some time—the company took action. This event led to the creation of a weekly meeting between the sales and marketing VPs. Not only did this simple meeting workaround prevent future disconnects, but it also gave rise to a creative new program that Data General used to market a new type of very thin computer server, its first "blade server." Marketing had pizza-delivery boxes made as packaging for the new servers, which were considerably smaller than previous servers, and had them delivered to IT directors. The unique packaging got the boxes opened, and the message that your servers could now fit in a pizza-delivery box captured the imagination of prospective buyers. Sales appreciated the calls this time around!

IT ALL COMES DOWN TO COMMUNICATION

It's probably apparent from these examples that the one common thread in generating effective workarounds between silos is to get together and talk about the issue. Of course, how you talk about it is just as important as what you talk about. When people get agitated or frustrated with someone, a common complaint emerges from their mouths: "What the heck are you *doing*?" Whether screamed or muttered, as obvious as the plaintive question may seem, it is nonetheless the wrong question. The perfunctory answer will almost always be something along the lines of: "I'm doing what I think matters."

Rather than treating the other person, team, or group as your enemy combatant, you will gain better purchase by following Larry Senn's advice and assuming innocence. In all likelihood, these parties are making choices based on differences in understanding owing to causes such as different goals or differences in how they are being measured. Sometimes the challenge boils down to the struggle detailed in Chapter 2—that of being overwhelmed, with more to do than can be done.

Arranging a meeting to talk about the issue makes sense in most instances. If you need to engage a given person, group, or department in order to get something moving, it may be most helpful if you start by asking yourself what the purpose or focus of the other party's job is. That should quickly put you on the path toward understanding that you each have different versions of a good outcome.

WORKAROUND QUESTIONS

Here are some questions to ponder before approaching parties who are causing a roadblock; these same questions may also help shape the discussion once you get together:

1. What is their job?

2. What is the purpose of their job, group, or department?

3. What does a good outcome look like to them?

4. How does their choice make sense from their point of view?

   • How are they being measured in terms of performance?

5. What is the purpose of your job, group, or department?

    - What is a good outcome from your point of view?

    - How are you being measured in terms of performance?

6. Are there common elements that you can emphasize to help bridge any gaps?

7. How does your work impact their work?

8. Is there anything you can do to make it easier for them to produce what you need?

9. Is there anything you can do to make it easier for them to produce what they need?

8

When Cultures Clash

When two organizational cultures collide, the aftermath can include differences of both style and substance. Cultural clashes can occur between companies doing business together and can even occur within a single company when departments function differently. What makes cultural differences so challenging is the not-so-obvious fact that culture is just the way things are inside your organization. Rarely does anyone think about how that culture operates; people simply live and conduct business inside it. In many respects, culture is the water in that old Zen saying, "The last thing a fish notices is water."

When cultures clash, rather than saying to one another, "It looks as if we perceive or do things differently," most people think the other group is somewhere between nuts and deliberately difficult. There are countless stories of differences that provoke clashes. For instance, large companies partnering with much smaller ones are sources of memorable culture-clash tales. When the large company interacts with the smaller company, rarely are the people from the large company even aware of their effect on the smaller company.

A couple of years ago, I was asked to help a large pharmaceutical company iron out some differences with its much smaller lab partner. The lab company employed fewer than 100 people and had a promising drug in development in a single location. The pharmaceutical company employed more than 20,000 people spread around the globe. The large company had more people assigned to the partnership than the lab had employees. You can foresee where this one is bound.

The pharma employees were forever calling people at the lab, asking for meetings, briefings, and data. Each call, meeting, or data-gathering expedition meant that lab employees were taken away from their lab work to serve the appetite for information of their larger partner. Endless meetings and requests for data were normal operating procedures for the large pharma company. Very formal, very hierarchical, glacially slow. The denizens of the small lab company were more accustomed to peeking in on someone in his or her office or lab, asking a quick question, and then returning to the job. Very informal, very flat, very quick.

Just about the time the pharma team would get up to speed, the organization would begin another round of job rotations. Pharma staff would then cycle off the partnership and rotate to other jobs within their behemoth organization—all part of their normal career-development process. That meant another load of new pharma staff with their own need for briefings, meetings, and unique data and information. People at the pharma company never noticed, much less understood, the negative impact they were having on the lab company. But they were quick to complain about how long it was taking to get the drug through development.

After interviewing a sampling of people on both sides, I arranged for a one-day off-site working session in which they could train their attention on their joint objective of getting this promising drug developed, approved, and into the commercialization stream. They explored their unique contributions to the process and what each side needed from the other in order to move forward. We also delved into the operating styles of each company.

Once both sides understood the needs of the other as well as what the cultural norms were for the other company, they were able to come up with a few workarounds that were meant to streamline things. Workarounds included the development of a common database where new pharma partnership staff could go for information, as well as a briefing process for people newly staffed to the partnership. However, the pharma culture was built around meetings and e-mail, which meant that the database rarely was accessed. Moreover, as people were reassigned, their attention flagged, and they not only failed to populate the database but also lost interest in attending briefing meetings.

It is unfortunate but true that not all workarounds actually work: the project stalled, the large pharma became impatient, and the partnership eventually came undone. In this instance, the arrangement would have worked better if the large pharma had assigned a dedicated team to the project and colocated that team in one setting with the lab. That would have allowed members of the pharma team to have the knowledge and intimacy they required but without the revolving door of people coming into and out of the project. The dedicated team would have then been able to filter information back to the parent company without having to constantly distract the lab team.

Another lesson learned from this project is one that I call "nightmare scenario planning"—that is, sometimes workarounds have their own built-in risks for which another workaround may be necessary! Planning for the possibility that the workaround itself will break down turns out to be pretty smart.

The next time this kind of situation arose, I had the two teams think about possible solutions, and once they proposed something, I had them brainstorm all the possible land mines that could interfere with the outcome. As it turns out, it's not too hard for teams to project nightmares and possible solutions. All you have to do is ask them:

1. Have you ever seen anything like this solution before?

2. Has this kind of solution experienced trouble in the past?

3. What might cause this kind of project to go off the rails?

4. Does this project have any of those kinds of vulnerabilities?

5. What could we do this time around to lower the risk?

6. What recovery process could we put in place should it blow up anyway?

Next, we will look at two biotech companies partnering in an area with vast commercial opportunity and competitive advantage in light of how early they were to the market. As you will see, they managed to squander a considerable portion of their advantage by failing to understand differences between the two companies and their cultures.

CULTURE CLASH PART 1: COMMERCIAL CONFLICTS

Two biotech organizations formed a partnership to deliver on a large market opportunity. One company (Diagnostics) had extensive expertise in developing tests to detect certain diseases, while the other (Therapeutics) had a solid track record in developing treatments. Although the two companies saw some natural synergies between their products, they failed to see the sharp differences between the organizational cultures that guided how each operated. One culture was markedly hierarchical, which led to silos operating in isolation from one another. The other was a much more collaborative culture, in which cross-functional teams were formed to guide new products through development and into the marketplace. Their original partnership had been formed several years earlier, and the companies were first to the market with a significant product: a test, or assay, that detected a serious health threat, along with an effective treatment. However, as the two organizations moved down the road to expanding sales, they began to experience challenges in their business relationship.

Both sides had thought the initial contract was fine before they had a commercially viable product ready for the market. Over time, though, sales grew beyond initial expectations. Diagnostics employees began to think they deserved a heftier share of the revenues and became convinced that the terms were no longer fair. As their sense of having been wronged grew, they also became suspicious of the other, larger company and its motives. As previously noted, the larger company, Therapeutics Inc., had more experience in the actual development and commercialization of treatments, whereas the smaller company had more expertise in the development of tests. In line with typical marketing practices in the industry, the test and the treatment were well linked. As a consequence, the larger company endeavored to get closer to the smaller company in an effort to learn more about the test development and approval process.

The closer it got, the more Diagnostics began to suspect that Therapeutics was trying to learn how test development worked so that it could bring the capability in-house. In truth, Therapeutics wanted to learn more about the Diagnostics processes only so that it could pair its own product development with the test development in order to shorten time to market. As much as Therapeutics tried to assuage the fears of Diagnostics, tensions continued to mount, and each organization began to hinder the progress of the other. Over a several-year period, lawsuits had been filed, arbitration processes had been entered, and the companies had become increasingly adversarial.

As the tangle worsened, both companies resorted to enlisting legal teams to try to sort out various conflicts around commercial terms, regulatory approval, clinical affairs, and product development. Each side had its own processes and procedures, which it vigorously defended. Eventually, they reached an impasse, with another arbitration process on the verge of moving to the courts for resolution. The constant delays were allowing competitors to catch up, and large chunks of market share were being lost.

As is often the case, the initial discussions had centered on how blending their different capabilities might lead to commercial advantage. Had the two companies also spent some time on their internal processes, decision making, information sharing, and the like, they might have arrived at a more workable agreement. If they had also employed a version of the nightmare scenario planning mentioned earlier, they might have easily identified some underlying trust reservations that could have been ameliorated early on. It was later revealed that Diagnostics had a few key managers who were deeply suspicious of all large companies, while Therapeutics assumed from the outset that its commercial development experience would naturally give it the deciding voice when the partners had differences of opinion.

Workaround: Bring in a Neutral Third Party

Therapeutics was on the cusp of throwing the whole thing to the lawyers, when a senior member of the team called my company to ask for advice. The conversation started out with looking for ways to influence Diagnostics. We turned the tables by asking what Therapeutics thought the problem looked like from the Diagnostics point of view. After a series of questions, it became increasingly clear that as intransigent as Diagnostics appeared to be, so too were several key players within Therapeutics.

The conversation shifted from "how do we change them?" to "how do we change ourselves?" This was by no means the first time we had to help a company realize that the first change it needed to make was internal. The Therapeutics challenge was one of both control and influence; the company had a few levers it could pull that might prove useful, but in order to pull them it had to first influence its own key players to think and behave differently.

What started out as a question of how to work around the other company evolved into a series of questions about how to work around its own internal issues and perceptions. Therapeutics needed to address hardened positions that had developed among its groups. The Regulatory Affairs, Clinical Affairs, and Commercialization groups had all begun telling themselves different versions of the same story about how the other company was lost in the jungle.

We helped them analyze the issues from the perspective of Diagnostics, including what kind of evidence Diagnostics might be looking at to support its contention that it had been taken advantage of and how its contributions were being minimized. It didn't take much exploration for Therapeutics executives to realize that they had behaved in a typical large-company fashion, thinking only of their own interests and not taking the time to understand how various terms and conditions might be perceived by or might actually inhibit the other side. Once their own groups saw the possible implications, they were able to soften their positions enough to entertain a more open exploration with the other company.

At the suggestion of Therapeutics, both companies agreed to bring in outside help in the form of negotiation and alliance expertise. As part of the outside assistance, both companies sent their key executives to an off-site location, and together, the two teams underwent two days of negotiation training, developing a deeper understanding of win-win mind-sets and processes.

Of the original dozen contentious issues, all but one was resolved during the weekend retreat. The lone remaining issue concerned revenue splits stemming from the initial contract, and the two CEOs agreed to take this one themselves. A couple of weeks later, the revenue debate had been resolved as well, and the two teams were back to collaboration, jointly facing the competition rather than treating each other as the competitor.

The good news: they were back in the game. The not-so-good news: the time spent in adversarial spats over the previous three years had allowed a competitor to finish development of its own assay and treatment. From a virtual 100 percent share of the market, the partners now had 60 percent. The net impact? About $40 million per year in lost revenue.

CULTURE CLASH PART 2: BETTER TO BE RIGHT OR RICH?

While this particular workaround did blunt the main point of contention, it did not really clear up some of the underlying trouble spots that had precipitated the conflict. Perhaps our fascination with quick fixes is at the root of many of our problems. In the case of Therapeutics and Diagnostics, once the contentious contractual matters had been settled, the two companies moved forward in examining a couple of new public health issues for which they were well positioned.

Meanwhile, the two organizations had not really identified the ground-level trust issues, and more challenges soon developed. This time, however, the challenges were not due to the business arrangement; differences in culture were the source of friction. The cultural differences had been there all along, but the two senior teams had been satisfied to tackle the contract complaints without looking at the substantive differences in how the two companies operated.

Therapeutics had developed an internal culture of collaboration. Management routinely rotated across functions and business units, which yielded a broad range of experience and insights across the various areas of the business. Over time, Therapeutics employees had become accustomed to encountering differing points of view and had learned how to collaborate with other internal groups.

Diagnostics, though smaller and younger, was characterized by a much more hierarchical management structure out of which had emerged several somewhat isolated silos. Within Diagnostics, Regulatory Affairs and Clinical Affairs were part of a single group whose job it was to navigate FDA approvals for the assay. Product Development was its own silo and generally took over once certain FDA approvals had been granted.

Over at Therapeutics, Regulatory, Clinical, and Product each had its own management, but because of the collaborative nature of the organization, each had become accustomed to seeking and accepting input from the others. With this seemingly innocuous difference in organization, the partnership embarked on developing an assay and product for a newly emerging public health issue. Both organizations agreed that they would seek to "fast-track" the development, testing, and approval process.

The goal was to utilize a process that had been developed for an earlier product, although the earlier product and the current product had different indications (conditions that make a particular treatment or procedure advisable). Because the indication was different, the FDA would be scrutinizing the application, and in two different areas: how well the assay worked in terms of detection and how effective the treatment was for the indication.

Diagnostics was much more familiar with the approval process for detection versus the process for efficacy or downstream commercialization, given that it makes and markets assays, not treatments. Therapeutics understood the detection approval process somewhat but had considerable knowledge about what would be required to gain approval for commercialization. The collaborative style of Therapeutics produced a series of recommendations for their Regulatory and Clinical Affairs counterparts at Diagnostics intended to help speed up the approval for eventual commercialization.

Can you guess the conflict that was about to emerge? Members of the combined Regulatory and Clinical groups at Diagnostics were not interested in the collaboration offered by Therapeutics, viewing the offer to help as interference. In addition, the original suspicions that Therapeutics harbored a desire to usurp the capabilities of Diagnostics lingered within the Regulatory Affairs organization.

Members of the Product Development team at Diagnostics well understood the challenges and solutions being presented by Therapeutics. However, given the hierarchical and silo nature of the company, they were not provided a seat at the table. The director of the combined Regulatory and Clinical groups "owned" the process and was not about to let anyone else into his playground.

The result? The FDA approved the detection assay but withheld the approval for commercialization. That led to another series of fierce fights between the two companies, with each blaming the other for the outcome. Diagnostics claimed that all would have been fine had it not been for the distractions and interference, while Therapeutics claimed that all approvals would have been granted had its advice been followed and the nature of the clinical trials adjusted to include the all-important effectiveness proof.

In hindsight, Therapeutics realized that it was not getting its messages heard because of the walls in place between Regulatory and Product Development at Diagnostics. Therapeutics had been taking its message to the wrong group; had it gone to Product Development, the message would have been understood. Still, given the walls between the silos, even that might not have been sufficient to get the minor changes made that would have garnered full approval for both detection and commercialization.

It took another sequence of CEO-to-CEO conversations to get the message understood within Diagnostics. The companies did manage to conduct a second round of testing following the advice from Therapeutics, and the product eventually received FDA approval to go to market.

All told, the delays put them into the market two years late, resulting this time in $80 million in lost revenues. The number grows even larger when you factor in how much market share they surrendered while having to repeat the clinical trials.

Some high-profile players wound up losing their jobs, and the trust between the two companies continued to erode.

Workaround: Plan for Differences

If you are trying to influence a person, a department, or even a company, it is imperative that you understand what is driving the other's behavior. What matters to this party, and why does it matter? What if there are differences in how the two of you plan? How does each party make decisions? Who gets to be involved?

Heed the lessons from Therapeutics and Diagnostics: culture matters! Rather than assume that some other group will behave the way your group behaves, you should assume that there may be differences and plan accordingly.

In this instance, Therapeutics was eventually able to influence Diagnostics after conducting what the company now calls a "constituency analysis." Others may call this a stakeholder analysis. You, in turn, could say, "People do things for *their* reasons, not *my* reasons."

While thinking more about the underlying interests of their counterparts at Diagnostics, managers at Therapeutics also learned a basic lesson about understanding how the other company is organized, who runs which groups, and who is likely to be impacted by the joint effort. Once they had this basic understanding in place, the next thing they needed to do was meet with key managers (stakeholders) to find out what was important to each group and how decisions got made internally.

Here, the hierarchical nature of the organizations led department heads to jealously guard their turf and do whatever they could to claim credit for advancement or success.

Therapeutics managers began to understand that their own preference for collaboration ran counter to the command-and-control nature of their partner and the autonomy of key silos. Armed with this insight, they then briefed their CEO on the issues and what would likely be required to move forward. From there, another CEO-to-CEO meeting took place. Therapeutics acknowledged that understanding and support for its commercialization suggestions would naturally lie within the Diagnostics Products organization and that the two CEOs would need to figure out a way to get the Diagnostics team on board.

A few meetings later, and after some internal due diligence, the Diagnostics CEO, true to the command-and-control nature of the company culture, issued instructions to the various groups about how they were to proceed, and the process was back on track.

HOW DO YOU DEAL WITH DIFFERENCES?

Cultural differences can exist between departments or geographic locations within the same organization as well as between different companies or partners. One of the major challenges presented by cultural differences is that we rarely call the differences something as bland as "differences."

When we label the differences as something difficult, wrongheaded, or just plain ignorant, we begin to view others as adversaries. As in the case of the two biotech companies, differences in approach can lead players to impute negative motives to the other side.

In all likelihood, your job requires you to interact with other groups or departments within your company, perhaps with external companies as well. Each group or department has developed ways of doing things that to its members seem natural and correct. Those ways of doing things could be very different from how your constituency does things, even if you are both in the same industry or are theoretically doing similar jobs. If you are noticing some differences in approach or style, you could benefit from taking some time to assess how you operate similarly and how you operate differently. From there you can engage in a conversation with the other group to make certain you are all on the same page.

WORKAROUND QUESTIONS

Sometimes a workaround can be discovered or at least anticipated before the roadblock ever darkens the path. If you are partnering with someone, here are some questions to consider before launching or lurching down the path. These questions apply equally well to partnerships between two people, between two teams within the same company, and between two companies. You may need to explain that exploring these questions might seem like covering old ground but that what you are really doing is checking to see if you both are on the same page and have the same understanding of expectations and operations.

1. What is your common intention or purpose?

   - What are the drivers and key interests of the other group?

   - What are your drivers and key interests?

   - Are both sets of drivers and interests aligned, in conflict, or just different?

   - What risks are each of you trying to protect against?

2. What are your important goals and outcomes?

   • Which goals and outcomes are shared?

   • Who else is going to care about this besides you and your direct partner?

   • What are the unique goals and outcomes for each party?

3. What areas of focus and responsibility do you each have?

   • Should you each have rights to consult with the other on decisions or processes?

4. Have you seen anything like this work well in the past?

   • Are there any lessons or practices that you should consider for this effort?

5. Have you seen anything like this get in trouble in the past?

   • What should you do if problems or disagreements arise?

9

Death by Decision: Stop Deciding and Start Choosing

What is it about making decisions that seems so darn difficult? You know as well as I that even simple decisions on the home front about where to go to dinner or what movie to see can become crippling:

"Want to go to dinner tonight?"

"Sure. Love to."

"Great. Where would you like to go?"

"Oh, I don't care. You choose."

"Wait a minute—I chose last time."

Sound at all familiar?

As you read through this chapter, consider situations in which you were stuck in a difficult decision-making process while various team members were trying to find the perfect solution. The pursuit of perfection can often get in the way and lead to participants arguing what's right or wrong with any particular set of options, all the while striving to arrive at a perfect, durable, never-changing decision.

Even if your team somehow managed to settle on that timeless, durable, perfect decision, I'll bet circumstances eventually arose that caused that initial decision to be scrapped. To avoid playing out these losing hands, what can you do when your team gets bogged down in arguing about perfect solutions or perfect decisions? In Chapter 3, I cited two critical questions for senior teams when my company begins a new assignment. The first question: "What is the vision, mission, or purpose of this organization?" The second question: "What are the top three strategic objectives for the coming 12 to 18 months?" When I work with teams to clarify purpose, vision, goals, objectives, and metrics, and we finally reach alignment on both direction and outcomes, I then ask one more critical question: "What will you have to be good at in order to succeed?"

That means both "you" personally and "you" as the executive team. I'm not asking what the direct reports, departments, teams, or units will have to do well; I'm asking what the executives themselves will have to be good at in order for the larger organization to succeed. In virtually any size of organization, many of the same issues seem to arise again and again. Communication, information sharing, and timely decision processes usually top the list. While other concerns typically are voiced as well, such as risk management and staffing, the need for streamlined decision making is almost always near the top. Knowing how agonizing it can be to make even inconsequential decisions about dinner or movies, it's not hard to account for decision avoidance in the workplace. However, anything that impedes decision making can have ripple effects all over the place.

Sales can't take to the field without clear direction on strategic product lines to emphasize; operations can't gear up to manufacture without specs and forecasts; marketing can't launch campaigns if targets aren't clear; HR can't recruit and train without guidance on resource needs and constraints. Leadership must not only be decisive in selecting its strategic directions but also be decisively clear about the directions in which it is not going. Dave Logan, author of *Tribal Leadership*, told me, "Leaders need to kill off alternatives" so that the organization is clear about where it is going and not going. That way, you'll avoid second-guessing yourself and revisiting the same decision repeatedly. It's a straightforward process: define your purpose, clarify your outcome, pick your direction, and get going. However, you should also allow for the fact that sometimes things don't go as planned.

There is a subtle difference here between choosing an option and killing off the others. As Dave Logan points out, many organizations choose an option and then keep revisiting the others. In the kinds of situation he references, decisions keep being revisited because some people refuse to accept the decision and wish to keep rehashing it. That endless loop can be debilitating, and in that sense, he is correct in advising that leadership "kill off the alternatives."

Once a choice has been made, let's all get behind it and start implementing the chosen solution. In this instance, "kill off the alternatives" means stop the endless debate and get busy. It does not mean kill them off in the sense of labeling them wrong or invalidating their possible advantages in the future. It simply means having the clarity to declare a choice and implement it.

If the chosen alternative proves not to work, then the previously discarded options can be brought back into the discussion—not because the decision is constantly being second-guessed, but because data or events show that something different is needed.

WHY DECIDING IS SO PAINFUL

What follows is a glimpse into what passes for decision making in many organizations, an approach that rarely is as bold and decisive as it is negative. There is a great difference between choosing an alternative and then moving forward versus declaring alternatives wrong and limping along with what's left.

Decision Scenario 1: Analytically Impossible

Imagine you are in a meeting, the goal of which is to make a decision. The group has in front of it three options from which to decide a future direction. The moderator asks the group for thoughts about option A. Mary starts to extol the virtues of option A, when Bob jumps in and points out its flaws, limitations, and other inadequacies. The moderator duly notes that there are certainly some serious concerns about option A and turns her attention to option B. A similar pattern emerges, with a few comments in favor and another deluge of critical comments about why option B will never work.

All right then, how about option C? There are two categorically different types of groups that could be present in this meeting. A technically oriented group may devolve into deeper analysis and ever more data, offering a few arguments in favor and another host of reasons why option C won't work either. At this point, the group may become paralyzed and conclude that there really isn't anything that can be done. (Someone in this instance is likely to mutter, "I told you there isn't anything to be done. What a waste of time.")

Decision Scenario 2: The Last Choice Standing

Again, a group has convened to make a decision with the same three options to weigh. A similar pattern emerges, with options A and B being proposed, supported, and then shot down.

This group knows it must do *something*, and the first two options have already been dismissed. That leaves only one standing. If you have ever been in this scenario, you know what comes next. The moderator says something like: "Well, team, with A and B already dead, it looks as if the only thing we can do is enact option C." And everyone agrees. Option C does not get the same scrutiny as A and B because, after all, we have to do *something*.

If the team members pick the last remaining option and try to force it into action, what will they do if the option shows signs of not working? "Try harder!" "Get committed." "Focus!" These are the common admonitions of the leader who "decided" that the last remaining option was the only way to go, especially if this leader had been among those arguing why A and B were inadequate. Just think about it: what would happen if this leader acknowledges that option C isn't working and returns to option A or B instead? This kind of about-face could be seen as admitting weakness, that the leader was "wrong" in the first place. Definitely career limiting in some organizations!

The problem in both scenarios lies in what the participants were asked to do—they were asked to *decide* rather than to *choose*. What's the difference? Let's start with *decide*, or *de-cide*. Do you know any other words that end in *cide*? How about the following list:

Sui-cide

Homi-cide

Patri-cide

Matri-cide

Fratri-cide

Geno-cide

Insecti-cide

I'm sure you can see the pattern. The suffix of these words derives from a Latin root that basically means "to cut, kill, or tear apart." Another meaning is "to stumble accidentally into a snare." No wonder people avoid decisions! Who wants to be involved in killing things? Even more frightening, who wants to risk stumbling into a snare or being torn apart? As we noted, if you just spent hours killing off options A and B, thus leaving you with either no way forward or plowing ahead with C, you may be in a real pickle if C doesn't prove itself to be workable. The more energy we invest in declaring what's right and what's wrong, the more debilitating reality becomes if we turn out to have missed something along the way. It's pretty hard for most people to do an about-face, admit their mistakes, and take back their strenuously made arguments.

It's even more challenging if the decision process involved tearing apart ideas submitted by team members. If you are obliged to revisit the decision, you may also have to revisit the team members who have been torn apart. You don't have to be especially astute to have noticed that a good number of people operate out of "don't-stick-your-neck-out" kind of thinking. Once someone has been torn apart for his or her brainstorming ideas, it's not a stretch to imagine that person staying in the background.

Decision Scenario 3: Choosing Toward Your Desired Outcome

If asking people to decide isn't such a dandy idea, what's a better one? *Asking them to choose.* The word *choose* comes from the Latin word meaning "to taste," and current definitions include "to have a preference for," "to select freely," and "to take an alternative." Have you ever asked for a taste at the ice-cream store or the wine bar before selecting something? Tasting first can help you figure out if you want to go that route or perhaps try something else instead.

I like to think of *choice* as implying a sense of freedom and direction while moving toward something, whereas *decide* suggests moving away from something (cut out, avoid the snare, kill off). It's a whole lot easier to get somewhere by moving toward the target than by moving away from something else. If we ask the team to choose, rather than to decide, the discussion might be slightly different. "Let's examine these three choices—how might each of them help us get to our desired outcome? How well equipped are we to successfully implement each choice?"

As the team considers each option, it will come up with a choice that appears most likely to result in success for any number of *positive* reasons, rather than the *negative* reasoning of what is wrong with each choice. Imagine that the team members have selected B because they feel best equipped to implement it. A or C could work, although both would require resources and skills that aren't as well developed as those required for B.

Suppose they discover later on that B isn't working as they hoped. Now what? If they had *decided* that A and C were hopeless, there is no turning back; they either push on or declare defeat. However, had they simply *chosen* B without having killed off the other options, it would be possible to revisit A and C to check if one of them now makes more sense. Or, having learned something from implementing B, the team may regroup and discover elements of A or C that could be incorporated into B or discover other options that have become apparent along the way. You could think about this approach as something similar to continuous improvement.

Most decision processes ask people to argue vigorously for "the right way forward." Those arguments often contain elements of attack directed at options. The real goal of decision making, what we are calling "choice" here, is not about being right; it's about being effective. If you can *choose toward a desired outcome* rather than kill off all other possibilities, you may then have the freedom to learn, to course correct, and to keep making progress as new data and experience are acquired.

ONCE YOU HAVE CHOSEN . . .

It's important to be abundantly clear about not only which direction you are taking but also which directions you are *not* taking. That doesn't mean you have to kill those alternatives in the sense that they are down and out forever, but you do need to be clear that those alternatives are no longer on the table.

Here's a simplistic example of the difference between deciding and choosing: if you have three flavors of ice cream from which to choose, and you choose vanilla, does that mean you can never, ever choose chocolate or strawberry? Or imagine you're serving fish tonight and choosing between a chardonnay and a pinot noir to accompany it. Let's say that you are of the mind that the chardonnay will go better. Does selecting chardonnay mean that you can never choose pinot noir from this day forward? What if you find out that it doesn't work quite the way you like? Should we argue about which is the one and only right choice? If you "decide" that chardonnay is the one and only "right" wine, do you then destroy all the pinot noir? (By the way, many sommeliers will point out that pinot noir, a red wine, goes extremely well with salmon, despite the conventional wisdom that white wine should be served with fish.)

If you have a clear purpose and intention, supported by a defined set of outcomes, you can gear up to achieve your mission. Clarity around intended outcomes and a pathway forward should then provide you a way of measuring progress and help you assess possible detours along the way.

If you keep marching forward, and the results fail to material-ize, you may need to revisit alternatives that were left behind. However, that is not the same as constantly revisiting discarded alternatives while trying to make progress on the one selected.

Some people will keep raising alternatives even as the team tries to move ahead. If you are part of a consensus-driven organi-zation, this kind of "what if" questioning is guaranteed to grind things to a halt while every decision is revisited and then revisited again. As time passes, progress toward the desired outcome loses any glimmer of hope, and the "what if" member of the team gets to claim a Pyrrhic victory—the solution agreed-upon no longer works, and he or she gets to tell everyone, "I told you so."

Another version of resistance raises its ugly head after a deci-sion has been reached and a choice made with no apparent dis-agreement from those attending. People congratulate one another on the productive meeting and good outcome, and they begin to take action. It's only then that a dissenting voice rises, challenging the course of action, claiming nothing had been approved. As with the "what if" scenario, a consensus-driven organization will grind to a halt at this point, replaying the meeting and decision, often with the same result.

Both of these cycles can be replayed as though on a continuous loop until someone exercises a handy workaround, one that will work for either scenario: documentation. This workaround is both preemptive and responsive. Whether it is your meeting or not, send out clear meeting notes afterward documenting decisions made, following a regular format. If you provide clarity of purpose beforehand, and then document the outcome, you may be able to put the constant raising and reraising of issues to bed.

The best practice is to review what will be going into the meeting summary before everyone leaves the meeting and to ask for dissenting opinions at that time. A recommended meeting summary should include:

- Date of meeting

- Purpose of meeting (issues discussed or resolved)

- Those invited

- Those attending

- Alternatives discussed

- Alternative(s) selected

- Any metrics in place, goals, etc.

- Any specific projects agreed upon

- Who has what roles, rights, or responsibilities going forward

- Next actions

- State that absent dissenting opinions, these stand as the agreed-upon outcomes of the meeting and the decisions taken

You can always take the lead, share your answers to the questions above, and then ask for any additions or corrections right then and there.

THE INSANITY CALAMITY

We have all heard the definition of *insanity* as doing the same thing over and over again, expecting a different result. One reason we see so much apparent insanity in day-to-day life could be traceable to people making decisions from a negative stance (away from something) rather than the more positive act of making choices toward desired outcomes.

Negative decision processes as described in scenarios 1 and 2 earlier in the chapter can lead to endless loops of "trying harder" coupled with defensiveness or the need to prove someone "right" by trying to force a previous "square peg" decision into a "round hole" issue. In scenario 1, everyone killed off the ideas on the table, and so the team was left with "business as usual."

In scenario 2, the team selected option C because it was the only one left standing after A and B were assassinated by the process of de-ciding. If the team moves downstream and option C proves to be even more problematic than the other two, the team leader often goads the troops to try harder or get committed, desperate to pull off an unlikely success. But that's only because other options have already been killed off—there's nowhere left to turn.

Both scenarios 1 and 2 give way to differing versions of the insanity calamity—people trying to produce meaningful results from already failed options.

Workaround: Choose Toward Your Desired Outcome

If you find yourself or your team mired in a difficult issue, struggling to come up with an effective decision, why not abandon your agenda for deciding and go about choosing instead?

When faced with a difficult decision:

1. Determine your desired outcome, and clarify your intention for getting there.

2. Assess your capability to implement each of the available choices.

3. Make the best *choice* you can *toward the desired outcome.*

4. Remain open to new data that may cause you to reevaluate your choice.

Now, as long as you know the general direction, are committed to getting there, and have some decent ability to notice what's going on along the way, you can always choose to go with a version of an old joke, "Ready, fire, aim." Obviously, "Ready, fire, aim" is likely to get you into even more trouble than you started with. A better formula is the updated version: "Ready, fire, steer." In today's "smart weapons" technology, "Ready, fire, steer" is the operative concept. Part of "ready" means clarifying the purpose or desired outcome (destroy the mobile device that is firing on us), "fire" means launch the "smart weapon" with sufficient data about the intended target, and then let the weapon system "steer" toward the moving target.

All too often, we start with only limited information about our purpose and intended outcome, and then we become frozen in place by our desire to map out all the contingencies and action steps necessary to get there. Perhaps what we really need to do in those circumstances is to remain homed in on the goal, take the next step in that direction, and reassess as we notice the results en route.

Human beings have accomplished some impressive results with a form of this thinking. When Kennedy engaged the nation in putting a man on the moon, much of the required technology did not yet exist. The same was true when NASA turned its attention to launching the International Space Station, an endeavor that was predicted to require 30 years to complete.

"Ready, fire, steer" may be one way of thinking about the process that culminated with the space station in orbit. Initial clarity about the objective kept people on course, even though numerous technologies were tried, found wanting, and redeveloped. No one option could possibly have been mapped out in advance with precise detail. Instead, directionally correct thinking was the required mind-set, even though rocket scientists favor perfection when given a choice.

No matter where you are, there's always a next step, even if it appears more like backtracking. I know that backtracking can seem like a complete waste, but what are you supposed to do when you come up against a bridge that's out or when the weather grounds your flight?

IT'S A LOT EASIER TO STEER SOMETHING IN MOTION

Much as with driving a car, once you get something moving, it's a whole lot easier to steer. Of course, you do need to know something about your destination, or you'll just be driving in circles, wasting a lot of gas, getting nowhere.

Endless meetings with the aim of arriving at a perfect decision are a lot like driving in circles, burning a lot of gas and getting nowhere. If you get stuck trying to make a decision, the workaround I recommend is to let go of the need to get it right or perfect, and instead just get it moving. Most restaurants and ice-cream stores figured out the decision problem a long time ago. When confronted with multiple flavors of ice cream or multiple wines by the glass from which to choose, some customers get flustered and resort to old standbys, or they take the risk of picking something that they may not like.

Clever providers encourage the customer to ask for a taste, even several tastes, in order to facilitate the choice. No need to get it right up front—just choose something to sample, and if that doesn't work, pick something else. This kind of opportunity to sample first and choose later has allowed me to discover tastes that I never would have tried before. My wife at first found this tendency of mine to ask for tastes embarrassing. Now we both enjoy the experience, have learned a lot, and have broadened our frontiers.

WORKAROUND QUESTIONS

Whether or not you choose to reframe decision making as choice making, there are a few questions that may be helpful in making your choice or decision. Here's a good starter set of questions many people have found useful:

1. What is our purpose or mission as a company?

2. What is the issue that we are trying to solve?

3. How does this issue impact our customers?

4. How does this issue impact our unit, group, or team?

5. How does this issue impact other units, groups, or teams?

6. What outcome are we trying to achieve? What is our goal? Objective? What results will we produce?

   - How will we know if we get there? How will we review progress along the way?

   - Are there critical time lines, milestones, or due dates to be met?

7. What options do we have to get there?

   - How well equipped are we to execute the various options?

   - Which option makes the most sense based on current capabilities or capacities?

   - Do we have any current or anticipated conflicts, either internal or external?

8. What projects will we have to put in place to execute the preferred option?

   - What do we need to stop doing in order to proceed effectively and efficiently?

   - What do we need to continue doing, either in direct support of the project or because of good business practice?

   - What do we need to start doing as a result of this new direction, project, or goal?

9. What next actions will we have to take?

10. How will we know if we are on course?

11. What will we do if we find ourselves off course?

10

Moving Beyond Consensus

We have all heard the quip that a camel is a horse designed by committee. For people in some organizations, the camel would be a welcome outcome—at least there's some kind of animal coming out of that committee! Do you work in an organization that is driven by consensus? If so, then you may already be meeting'd to death. Consensus is one of those ideas that sound so logical when you hear it and then drive most people crazy when they try to implement it.

According to Merriam-Webster, *consensus* has the following meanings:

1a: general agreement: unanimity
1b: the judgment arrived at by most of those concerned
2: group solidarity in sentiment and belief

What's not to like about general agreement or group solidarity? The sticky part is in that little word *unanimity*.

I have worked with many organizations over the years that have made various attempts at consensus-based decision making. What usually transpires is what we discussed in the previous chapter: in most versions of consensus, whenever someone objects to a decision, it is fair game to resurface the issue. And to resurface it again. And again. The basic rationale is that everyone must be on board.

You may have personal acquaintance with something similar to one or more of the following examples:

- An insurance company tries to run everything as consensus, with the end result that people spend roughly 90 percent of their day in meetings. They also suffer from the meeting that produces the need for another meeting that produces a sub-committee that identifies even more people who need to be looped in. You can infer the impact this has on people who actually have to do something other than attend meetings all day long.

- An aerospace company had become so enamored with perfect science that just about anyone could stop any program by raising anything from a doubt to a possible improvement. These constant doubts and suggestions led to all manner of schedule delays and cost overruns. The need for consensus—and its close cousin buy-in—had become so ingrained in the culture that the company found that it needed to create a workaround to its own consensus culture in order to get programs moving again. It opted to create a special advanced-concepts unit to extract lessons from years of building satellites, so that it wouldn't have to rely on engineers coming into agreement each time they build a new version of an old concept. Employing this approach reduced the time to design and build one satellite from an average of more than five years to 27 months. Other companies in other industries have reaped similar gains by sidestepping the consensus mind-set and moving toward documenting and implementing their own internal best practices.

- A small training company wanted to move away from its founder-driven decision process and replace it with one based on consensus among key players. A leadership team of five was put in place with the requirement that the members agree on virtually anything they wanted to implement, from strategic direction to product development. The good news is that more people have more input; the bad news is that it now takes months to get simple decisions out the door. One witty member of the firm called the move to consensus the Productivity Prevention Process due to how long the group can discuss, study, mull over, meet, discuss, and discuss again before making even the humblest of decisions.

Consensus thinking could work if everyone really wanted to be on board, but that's not always the way it unfolds. A savvy individual who may prefer something different from the agreement reached knows that he or she can stall things by using the ploy of raising doubts or disagreements later. People hang back for all kinds of reasons. Some would prefer to keep doing things as they have always done them to avoid having to break comfortable routines. Others are concerned that they may look bad in the new system. Some want to slow things down when they disagree with a solution because of the possible impact on their budgets or head counts. Some are apprehensive that new processes will shine unwanted light on their own performance deficiencies. Some have purely political motives and are unwilling to let something move ahead and thereby allow a rival to succeed.

DECIDE, CONSULT, INFORM

In Chapter 1, we came across the security technology company that is virtually paralyzed by its culture of inclusion and consensus. Inclusion is a positive goal, and it does not have to be paralyzing. The same could be said for consensus, although most of my clients are hard-pressed to cite examples in which consensus truly works.

The difference between inclusion and consensus is important. You can bridge the inclusion and consensus gap in a way that invites appropriate involvement while still enabling the organization to move forward. The workaround for endless meetings is to clarify roles, rights, and responsibilities of those who would be involved.

My former colleagues at Vantage Partners, a distinguished negotiation and relationship management firm, used a "decision matrix" to streamline the involvement and decision process. A form of the decision matrix that I often recommend involves clarifying three specific roles in any decision process:

- Who has the ultimate authority to *decide* something

- Who has the right to be *consulted* prior to a decision's being made

- Who has the right to be *informed* of any decisions

By clarifying rights to decide, along with rights to contribute through consultation, you can differentiate roles and accelerate the process considerably. People with experience or expertise who should be consulted know that they have the opportunity to provide input while also being clear that they do not hold the rights to decide the final outcome. Those who need to be informed can relax in the knowledge that the process will provide them with decisions made so that they can go about performing their tasks later on.

This simple roles and rights clarification allows more streamlined meetings involving only those who need to contribute given the nature of each meeting. In consensus-driven organizations, it is common to cast a wider net for each meeting "just in case" someone may feel excluded or "just in case" we may need someone to attend. For most *consultation* roles, group meetings aren't even necessary, since the outcome can be achieved in one-to-one conversations.

FROM CONSENSUS TO ENGAGEMENT

One of my large health insurance clients is working to reposition itself in the industry. Developing a new strategic direction will impact every business unit and every functional group.

This organization has a history of including just about every-one in just about every decision. That has meant that people spend an inordinate amount of time in meetings discussing topics but not really making much headway in either creating solutions or arriving at decisions.

The company was going through a massive reorganization as a result of the new health care reform legislation, and many people were unsettled about their future roles. HR had an internal career-navigation website in the works to help with the changes, but it was stumbling along through meetings, committees, and every-thing short of literal tea leaf reading.

An HR manager noticed that HR was tackling too many issues at once and, being subject to the consensus-driven mind-set of the organization, also making way too little progress. He also noted that those involved in exploring any given issue were more prone to reading the executive tea leaves to try to predict if approval might be forthcoming rather than proactively establish-ing direction and options. All that this did was bring on more and more meetings with more and more speculation, which in turn meant that little was being offered to leadership to actually see or implement.

The manager decided to try a creative workaround regarding the development of the career site. He invited people who he knew were interested in the subject to establish an informal team to jointly develop criteria for the redesigned career-navigation site. In effect, he gathered a group of people who he thought would have the right to be *consulted* on what the site should include. The team members then drafted a skeletal project plan and went about the business of creating a comprehensive SharePoint site (an internal intranet location for sharing data and documents) to demonstrate how they envisioned the career site's working.

Once they had the site up and functioning, they presented it to the HR leadership group that would have the ultimate *decision* authority. They explained the functional design criteria that the informal team had jointly developed, noted who had contributed, and demonstrated how the site would work once approved. Leadership was able to see both the comprehensive nature of the design and the collaborative nature of its development. From there approval of its final release was practically a slam dunk.

The entire project was conceived, designed, and implemented within a matter of weeks, whereas the idea had been kicking around in various HR and business unit committees for months with not even a set of design ideas in place, let alone a functioning site. Rather than getting bogged down in trying to pinpoint everyone who might want to contribute to the design, the HR manager restricted the scope to those who had relevant expertise. Once they had the prototype up and garnered leadership approval, it was a short step to test the solution with people who were likely to be eventual users.

PROGRESS TRUMPS BUY-IN

Over and over, we hear the apparently sage advice that we need to create "buy-in" before proceeding on any new direction. In my experience, buy-in is a laudable concept that is also pretty much guaranteed to slow anything down, if not kill it outright. Buy-in, as pointed out earlier, is a close cousin to consensus. Consensus organizations tend to invite along anyone and everyone who may have two cents to toss into the discussion, while a buy-in approach seeks to gain support from just about everyone before moving forward. Organizations that crave consensus also tend to be the same ones that crave buy-in. The two processes both stymie progress by catching people in seemingly endless loops of discussions, meetings, and more discussions in an attempt to satisfy virtually every complaint or concern.

In the mid-1990s, the U.S. Air Force commissioned a new, powerful missile-defense weapon that would require the development of a complex new technology. The prime contractor, Airco, had extensive experience building aircraft, while Satco had equal experience building space vehicles. Their combined expertise looked like a perfect match for the new weapon system. The multibillion-dollar program initially targeted testing in the early

2000s and full deployment by 2009. As is often the case in the aerospace world, the program ran into numerous schedule delays, some related to the complex technologies involved and some having more to do with the challenge of getting large numbers of people on board with any solutions or changes.

The initial test finally took place in 2007, several years late, but at least it worked. The customer agreed to go forward but with both eyes fixed squarely on timing and budget for the second test. Skepticism abounded, and the primary contractor brought in Marcos, a gung-ho Satco program manager, to lead the second test effort. He was tapped not only because of his technical capability but also because of his boundless enthusiasm for the program and confidence in the ability of the joint team to find its way to the goal. Marcos was resolute in his commitment to get this second test across the finish line in a year.

Hiring this can-do program manager may be considered the first workaround for this promising but troubled program. With so much doubt surrounding the program, finding someone willing to take the lead with high levels of enthusiasm turned out to be a critical success factor. Even the Airco leader who brought him in was skeptical, but the leader realized that without the positive, committed mind-set of this enthusiastic program manager, nothing was going to get done.

Marcos was worried about gaining buy-in from his 30-person team, but he knew that he had to get cracking if he was going to get this program across the finish line. He also knew that if he became preoccupied with buy-in, he would likely be spending inordinate amounts of time trying to convince those who did not wish to be convinced, rather than making the rapid progress that the program demanded.

I encouraged the leader to enlist those who were already on board, or who were at least willing to do what they could, and then begin moving forward with a small but committed team. Skeptics can add great value in the kinds of challenging questions they raise; skeptics can also cause things to screech to a stop while their objections are considered and considered again.

An amazing thing happens when you make progress. The valuable skeptic, one who is initially skeptical but still open, sees the progress being made and jumps on board, often enthusiastically. As the real deadwood skeptics find their club member ranks shrinking and themselves increasingly isolated by their own negativity, they are faced with two choices: they either get on board or leave. Rarely do you have to fire these people; they go away voluntarily because it gets lonely without a supportive choir to keep preaching to. That's what happened here.

Marcos found a core team committed to producing a successful test, meeting or beating objectives regarding schedule, cost, and quality. Gaining commitment from a core team while the skeptics groused, complained, and did their best to demean both the team and the program leader wasn't necessarily an easy thing to do. Nevertheless, the core team agreed to go for it, moving aggressively forward to the one-year second test's goal.

Then, as they started to make progress, some of the skeptics started to become more engaged. With increasing engagement came increasing success, and the team crossed the finish line in one year and two days. Managers from both companies were thrilled, and the air force was ecstatic.

The "need" for buy-in can sound compelling, especially from rocket scientists. However, technically minded people can always expose one more wrinkle that needs to be studied, with the net result of slowing things down incredibly. Almost always, progress will trump buy-in, following the basic principle that nothing succeeds like success.

Sometimes the answer can be as direct as showing progress. If you are waiting for everyone to "buy in" on an idea, you may be retired before they all give the thumbs up. Instead, look for a few key players who are committed, determine what you can do on your own, and get on with it. Once you start showing progress, others will come around without much further discussion—a demonstration of the cliché that everyone loves a winner.

Remember: it's easier to ask for forgiveness than to get permission. If you keep asking for permission and seeking buy-in, you may merely be giving people reasons to object. A more productive method is to determine what needs to be done and then present those in charge with something completed rather than an idea that may need extensive discussion. It's a lot easier to produce that website, as the HR team did at the insurance company, and then make a couple of tweaks than it is to get the committee to come together to create the horse. Give your managers something they can see and touch, and you may have something that outweighs dissent or consensus.

WORKAROUND QUESTIONS

Here are some questions that should help you get around having to reach consensus:

1. Who will have the final decision authority for each decision type?

   • Who is ultimately accountable for the outcome?

   • Does the person or group accountable also have the necessary authority, resources, or support?

   • Does the person or group making the decision have the right input from the right groups in order to make a wise decision?

2. Who has the right to be included by being consulted?

   • Groups likely to be impacted financially by the decision

   • Groups likely to be called on for implementation support

3. Who has the right to be informed of the decision or outcome?

   • What performance requirements will they have?

   • What data will they need?

   • What authority will they need?

11

Are You a Corporate Firefighter?

Some organizations pride themselves on being exceptional at crisis management, aka firefighting. If you work for a fire department or some other kind of first-responder team, it certainly behooves you to be good at managing crises and putting out fires. Otherwise, that should not be the most important part of your job.

An IT manager for an investment bank told me recently that her department is forever being hit with calls from internal customers about matters requiring immediate response. Each call is the equivalent of someone's pulling the fire alarm and becomes an immediate call to action. The IT employees have become so good at responding to cries for help that two things are taking place, neither of which is good for the long run: they are getting more and more calls for help, and they are spending less and less time fixing the underlying causes. They enjoy the feeling of making a difference and actually look forward to those fire calls. They have assumed the role of firefighters.

Most good corporate firefighters complain in a somewhat prideful way about how much time they spend putting out those fires. Now, when was the last time you heard a real firefighter complain about putting out fires? Probably never, right? And why not? Well, it's the firefighter's job, isn't it?

Since many corporate fires are preventable, perhaps what is really needed is a good fire-prevention policy more than a good fire-response team.

WHEN IT SHOWS UP AND WHEN IT BLOWS UP

You probably know well the difference between important and urgent. Few corporate fires are both important and urgent, notwithstanding that once they have burst into flames, they take on the aura of both important and urgent. If you were to assume the role of arson investigator, you would probably discover that all kinds of fires had their origins back when the issue was confined—perhaps important, but with plenty of time to be addressed.

It's kind of like your passport or driver's license coming up for renewal. We all know the deadline is coming, and we also know it can be irritating to deal with the bureaucratic process, and so we put it off until later. Both renewals are important, yet neither starts out as urgent. Then "later" suddenly catches up with us. Maybe it's just before the trip for which you need the passport, or a day or two before your birthday and you notice that the driver's license is about to expire. Instead of spending a little bit of time filling out forms and submitting them for processing, you have to go into crisis mode, wasting a big chunk of time standing in lines and perhaps paying late fees.

If you have noticed that little things sometimes have a way of turning into big hooplas, then it may be worth examining how those little things were ignited. It's actually not so hard to discover: the answer lies somewhere between benign neglect and out of sight, out of mind.

Let's sift through a few common sources of the oily-rag-in-the-closet syndrome that produce more than their fair share of fires and crises. These examples can apply to corporate executives as well as support staff, to the small business owner, and right over to the single parent running the household.

WHERE FIRES AWAIT US

Many of our fires and crises erupt because we either keep putting them off, not unlike the driver's license renewal, or just don't see them. The ones we don't see are often buried someplace. Here are the three most common burial grounds:

- Your desk's in-box

- Your e-mail in-box

- Your head

You know you are snowed under when you have an in-box overflowing with stuff you have already seen once. Or twice. Or goodness knows how many times. True confessions, now: have you ever looked at something from your in-box, decided that you weren't sure what to do with it just now, and so put it back in the in-box? I know I have. I'll warrant most of us have. Unfortunately, that one little seemingly innocent act is a potential source of future fires and crises. By putting the piece of paper back in the in-box, we transform the in-box from a place for new information and communication to a combination in-box, storage device, and reminder system. Once the item is back in there, it's anybody's guess as to when it will reemerge. I suppose that depends on how often you go back and look at anything below the top couple of inches.

Take a stroll around your workplace and see how many in-boxes you can count that are empty. I'll bet there aren't many. Each full in-box could be an inadvertent hiding place for future fires. If you have put something back in the tray without deciding what action to take, you may not get around to it again before it's too late. Similarly, what if you have reviewed something and forwarded it on to Pat for some action he should be taking? And what if he reads it, returns it to his in-box, and assumes he'll get back to it "later"? And what if later winds up being too late?

These are the kinds of simple, innocent behaviors that can impel something small to turn into something requiring a fire drill. Even more frightening may be what we have stored in our heads! Have you ever seen something that needed response or action on your part and "made a mental note"? Where do you put that mental note, and when is it likely to surface again for action? If you're like me, you know that you will remember at some point; you just never know when. Perhaps it will be in the shower, just before falling asleep, or while driving the car.

Thanks, brain! The brain did its job—it remembered, just not so conveniently. Indeed, the brain will keep track—it's just that you never know when the mental note will show up again. How many times have you slapped your forehead and said something like, "Dang it! I knew this needed to be done. I forgot." Well, hey, "I forgot" is a pretty good excuse for another fire drill, don't you think? Probably not. So, what fire-prevention options do you have available to you? What are the fire-prevention options for avoiding starting your own fires, and what can you do to lower the likelihood that some other arsonist will start something for you to put out?

THE WEEKLY REVIEW: THE ULTIMATE IN FIRE PREVENTION

There's an uncomplicated workaround for this kind of situation, and it can work both for you and for the people with whom you interact. It's called the weekly review. As with many other situations, the workaround may require starting with yourself. In brief, the weekly review goes like this: once a week, review your calendar for the week that has just gone by and the one that is coming, to see if (a) anything fell through the cracks last week and (b) if anything critical is coming that warrants action today. You can review calendar entries, to-do lists, goals, projects, and commitments that you have made or that someone else made to you.

Action today could be anything from getting started on a project or goal of yours to reminding someone else that an important milestone, due date, or deliverable of some kind will be coming due. If anything got lost in the shuffle, you still have the chance to catch it while it may only be smoldering instead of waiting for it to erupt in a full-fledged fire. And if someone else let something slip, you can likewise catch it in the smoldering stage. By looking forward a week, you can position yourself to catch anything you spot or remind a team member, another department, or (heaven forbid) your boss that something important is coming.

This routine act of fire prevention is a great workaround and can go a long way to reducing the number of fires and crises that appear at your doorway. (If you have read *Getting Things Done*, you will already be familiar with this process.) Here's a no-sweat weekly review process that should help you extinguish any smoldering embers before a fire threatens to engulf the premises.

1. Get the number of items in your in-box to zero. (Using your in-box as a storage device is the equivalent of stashing oily rags in the closet. Pretty soon the heat will rise, and flames will roar!)

   a. Gather loose papers, notepads, and sticky notes containing information you need and place them in your in-box.

   b. Search through your in-box for anything in there that requires action of some kind.

   • Enter any actions that you discover on your Next Actions list. (You can think of this list as a more sophisticated to-do list: these are actions you need to take, more than results you need to produce. All results will have "next actions.")

   • Meeting notes can be hiding places for future fires. Did you take on responsibility for any actions at meetings this week that have not been entered on calendar pages or Next Actions lists?

2. Review the past week on your calendar for any items planned but not yet done. Did anything slip through the cracks? If so, do you need to do it now before it erupts into flames? If not, can you plan to do it next week?

3. Review the next week or two on your calendar for anything coming that you need to prepare for or even start now.

   a. If you need to prepare, do you have time scheduled for the preparation? If not, can you schedule that time now, even if it's for later today?

   b. Do you have anything due next week that you had better get started or you will run out of time? If so, when can you get it started? Do you need to calendar it?

4. Empty your head. Is there anything niggling in the back of your mind that you need to do, check on, or plan for? If so, does it belong on a Next Actions list, on a calendar page, or somewhere else besides your head?

5. Review project lists. If you don't have a list of projects you are responsible for, start one! Review each project on the list and confirm that you have an appropriate next action step and that it is being tracked in your system.

6. Review Next Actions lists. If you don't have a list of actions you need to take, start one! Assess each entry to see if either of the following conditions applies:

   a. You have already done it but did not check if off the list.

   b. It is getting close to urgent. If so, can you move it to your calendar and schedule it for action?

7. Review your Waiting For list. If you don't have a Waiting For list, start one!

   a. "Waiting for" items are kindling for major fires. Anything that you need to receive from someone else before you can continue with your part of the project or action is, by definition, a "waiting for" item.

b. Is there anything you need to ping someone else about to make certain the person has it moving? It's always best to look at least a week out so that any reminders you send along still have a chance of being acted on.

8. Review any checklists you have.

a. Do you have any items that you know you need to do each week? If so, can you take care of them now? For example:

- Pay bills.

- Back up your computer.

- Prepare any weekly reports.

9. Be creative and courageous. Is there anything you need to discuss with your boss? If so, can you schedule a meeting now?

Fires and crises are bound to occur from time to time; however, many fires break out because something simple but important was put off when it was still easy to address, just not urgent. Be careful that you do not start your own fires by casually putting off until later what you could handle now. Similarly, don't allow others to pour kerosene on your desk by their lack of attention to something that is important, just not urgent.

WORKAROUND QUESTIONS

The weekly review clearly will help your fire-prevention efforts on two major fronts: you will catch anything of your own that requires action as well as be able to identify threats that reside elsewhere. A hidden value of the weekly review is that if a fire does erupt, you will be better positioned to respond with a clear mind and full attention because you are already current on what's on your plate. Rather than responding to the fire with a nagging sense of "What am I forgetting?" you can take appropriate action and get back on track with less effort and less risk of having other fires erupt around you. Here's a recap of pertinent questions:

1. What projects and commitments do you have on your plate?

2. When was the last time you reviewed these projects with your boss to ensure that you are still on track with critical goals and objectives?

3. Are you tracking your projects and commitments separate from collecting them in your in-box or in your head?

4. Do you have separate lists or folders for projects, next actions, and anything you are waiting for that you can easily reference for reminders as well as for a quick scan if a fire does break out?

12

When the Best and Brightest Are Wrong

Perhaps you have heard of Garrison Keillor's popular public-radio show, "A Prairie Home Companion." In each show, he references Lake Wobegon, a mythical town in Minnesota. At the end of each broadcast, he signs off from Lake Wobegon, "where all the women are strong, all the men are good-looking, and all the children are above average."

THE LAKE WOBEGON EFFECT

The so-called Lake Wobegon effect has become increasingly present in schools and businesses, to the extent that many people actually believe that their entire organization is, in fact, above average. Such scholarly publications as *The Harvard Law School Forum* and the *Journal of Financial Economics* have reported on the impact of Lake Wobegon thinking.

The most common form of the Lake Wobegon effect can be recognized in the narrow thinking and hubris of key players in some corporations. Somehow, the notion that only the best ideas come from within seems to surface all over the place. Even an internally generated idea can run aground if it comes from the wrong person or group. This phenomenon has also been called the Not Invented Here (NIH) syndrome by many.

Over the course of my career, I have had the privilege of consulting for some of the most amazing companies on the planet. They all have at least one thing in common: all say they hire "the best and the brightest." No doubt the list of other companies that also claim to hire the best and the brightest is long and growing. Could the Lake Wobegon effect have any basis in the truth? How could everyone hire only the best and the brightest? How would you work around the hurdles that are inevitable when everyone is the rocket scientist's brain surgeon?

The road to ruin is laden with examples of what happens when hubris or NIH thinking runs the show. Here are just a few of them:

- Ken Olsen, founder and CEO of Digital Equipment Corporation, said in 1977: "There is no reason for any individual to have a computer in his home." I guess we can imagine what that mind-set did for internal innovation and product development.

- In the 1970s, the Swiss watch industry controlled 90 percent of the world watch market, utilizing mechanical movements made in Switzerland. In 1967, a Swiss research organization (Centre Electronique Horloger, in Neuchâtel) came up with the first quartz movement and offered it to the Swiss Watchmakers' Guild, an association of Swiss watchmakers. The Swiss watchmakers turned down the idea, and it eventually took hold in Japan instead. Seiko thought the idea had promise and used the quartz movement to assume a dominant position in the industry. One storied Swiss company went so far as to proclaim it would "never make a watch with a quartz movement." It later had to eat those words and now offers quartz movements. As the market gradually changed direction, the number of employees in member companies of the Watchmakers' Guild fell from some 90,000 in 1970 to a little more than 30,000 by 1984, while the number of companies decreased from about 1,600 to about 600 in the same time frame.

- In the early 1990s, Motorola was looking for opportunities within the cellular business as part of its technology growth strategy as well as examining possible competitive threats. Someone raised the question of how the company should view Nokia. The conversation quickly dissolved into snickering and jokes about this no-name company from Finland with a history of making everything from forestry products to bicycle tires to children's raincoats. By the mid-1990s, Nokia had divested itself of most of those businesses, choosing to focus exclusively on telecommunications. The snickering probably stopped by the time Nokia had surpassed Motorola as the global leader in mobile phones. By 2009, Nokia had a 38.6 percent market share, compared with 8 percent for Motorola. The snickering definitely stopped in July 2010, when Nokia acquired Motorola's telecommunications network equipment business. Oops.

It may well be true that "pride goeth before the fall."

"I WROTE THE BOOK ON THAT"

What do you do when you are stymied by the world's smartest person? What if the guy who wrote the book on the topic is convinced that he is right and you are wrong? Engineer Armando Martos found himself in exactly that situation once, and his story illuminates what happens when your great idea runs counter to that of the icon on the hill.

Armando was a freshly minted engineer when he landed a job at the Lawrence Livermore Laboratories. His very first assignment was to develop a design for a large (one meter in diameter and weighing 900 pounds) mirror mount. To help him through the process, the lab hired a well-known professor of kinematics from a major university as a consultant. Kinematics has to do with motion and the forces required to create the motion.

Armando studied the mirror mount requirements along with known challenges and then met with the professor to exchange ideas. When he returned a short time later with a few preliminary thoughts, the professor listened for a minute and then dismissed the ideas as unworkable due to some "basic" principles of kinematics.

Back to the drawing board, as it were, and after more study, Armando returned, still convinced that his ideas would work. The professor was not amused and this time gave Armando a copy of his well-regarded kinematics textbook to study. I'm sure you can sense the implied message here: *Look, I wrote the book on this—pay attention.* Armando dug into the book but, not being an expert in kinematics, did not see how to apply some of the formulas. After a couple more back-and-forth trips to the ivory tower, the advice was reduced to something painfully simple: "If you don't understand, just take my word for it. What you are proposing is the kinematic equivalent of the perpetual motion machine in physics. It's just not possible."

About this time, Armando's boss approached him to see how he was doing on the design. After sharing his frustrations, Armando learned that his boss had been getting the play-by-play all along from the professor. His boss offered two contrary thoughts: perhaps the professor was right, and he should give up; however, if Armando felt strongly about his ideas, he should go ahead and build a model to prove the concept.

Armando assured his boss that he knew the difference between stubborn and persistent. He also told him that if his idea worked, it would solve some of the most intransigent problems people had been experiencing for decades trying to come up with a stable yet unbinding design for large optics. His boss then told him to build the model and said he'd pay for it. Being a frugal tinkerer, Armando proceeded to build a crude prototype using door hinges, turnbuckles, and ball joints—the kinds of stuff he was used to seeing around his dad's truck repair shop (which is where he got the idea in the first place). And it worked!

Back to the ivory tower he went. Alas, not much had changed: the professor let Armando know how upset he was at him for wasting his time and the lab's money and commented that the only reason the model worked was that it was so crude. He went on to lecture Armando, stating that a precision model would never have been able to support the mirror. By now, Armando was ready to give up, but before doing so, he went back to the professor's book for one more careful read. This step yielded an incredible discovery: the professor was convinced the model wouldn't work because the professor was actually misapplying his own formulas! He had not seen a whole new degree of freedom that the new design provided and that was accounted for in the professor's own calculations. Indeed, the design worked both in theory and in practice.

Armando took this insightful discovery to his boss, telling him that he could easily prove that his idea worked, but not with his first crude attempt; it would require a more sophisticated model. His boss encouraged him to go for it and approved additional funding to produce the more refined model. Armando quickly produced a fully functioning model, and without even bothering to show his boss, he invited the professor to come down from the ivory tower and see the new model in action in his small office.

Ignoring the obvious signs of annoyance from the professor, Armando showed him how it worked and started to explain what he had learned from reading the professor's book. At that point, the professor put his hand up and asked Armando to stop talking. He spent 20 minutes staring at the model on the floor (it was large enough to occupy most of the office) without saying a word.

Armando remained respectful and uttered nary a syllable while the professor crawled all over the model. Eventually, the professor looked up and told Armando that he could never have imagined that Armando's model would work and asked him how he came up with the idea. As Armando took him through his thinking process and detailed how he had applied the professor's theories, the professor began to nod his head. For the first time in months, the professor spoke to Armando in respectful tones and acknowledged that he had discovered a whole new mechanism.

For Armando, having earned the respect of the professor was more important than having proved that his idea worked. That evening, Armando's boss caught up with him in the parking lot and asked how the meeting had gone. The expression on his boss's face was yet another level of acknowledgment that has remained with Armando for the ensuing 20 years. His boss then confided that he'd let Armando pursue the idea even though he didn't think it would work.

One year later, the professor called and asked if he could cite Armando in the third edition of his book; he was updating it and wanted to discuss the "Martos RSSR-SR Mechanism." Had Armando taken a direct assault position on the professor, attacking his misunderstanding or misapplication of his own theories, he probably would have been chucked out on his ear. A great lesson in both humility and influence can be taken from how Armando approached this situation.

FINDING A SOLUTION IS MORE IMPORTANT THAN BEING RIGHT

If you run into the roadblock of "the guy who wrote the book," try taking a page from Armando's experience. Remain respectful, ask for input, and see if you can cast the other person's idea in a form that allows him or her to maintain dignity. "Here's what I learned from you and how I applied your insight" may work a heck of a lot better than "Clearly, you don't understand your own area of expertise."

If you're more interested in finding a solution than appearing right or superior, you may well be able to apply the lessons that Armando so richly demonstrated:

- **Intention.** Armando has made a career out of several workarounds that work. First and foremost, he is a walking, talking affirmation of the power of intention. Get clear on where you are headed, and keep asking yourself what else you can do to get there. You may need to work around anything from self-doubt to the negativity or resistance of others.

- **Henry Ford workaround.** By staying resolute in his intention and his belief in the outcome, Armando was able to reach solutions. He is a living example of Henry Ford's previously quoted statement, "Whether you believe you can or you cannot, you are right." Despite the expert criticisms from the guy who wrote the book, Armando refused to accept "can't be done" without giving it a go. Not everything is going to work out, but you can be almost 100 percent assured that if you don't even try, it isn't going to happen.

- **Control and influence.** Armando recognized the situation and saw that there were things he could do on his own (study, build models, and apply theories). He also saw that he would need support to negotiate the hierarchy, so he showed his boss his personal initiative as well as his willingness to learn. The combination produced support even in the face of doubt. Never underestimate the power of taking control of your own 10 acres first. You will almost always move up a notch in the eyes of others by acting rather than complaining.

- **People do things for their reasons, not your reasons.** While it was clear to Armando throughout the ordeal that he had something that would work, he also knew that he would need to enlist his mentor/adversary/roadblock in order to bring it about. His repeated attempts to engage the professor were all framed in understanding what the professor had to say, not in proving that the professor was wrong. Even when he knew the professor had muffed the ball, he kept framing things in terms of the professor's theories. As hard as it might have been to accept that he had missed something, the professor could take comfort in the fact that his theories had worked after all.

WORKAROUND QUESTIONS

Here are some questions you should consider as you find your way forward:

1. What is the other person likely to think about your idea or approach?

2. How might the other person feel threatened or disrespected?

3. How can you use the other person's ability, position, or experience to move your idea forward? Can you show how your idea builds on his or hers? (People do things for their reasons, not your reasons.)

4. Who in the organization might serve as your mentor, advocate, or supporter, someone who can coach you in ways to present your ideas or influence the other person?

Workaround tip: remember that how you frame the problem is the problem. Stay focused on the solution more than how the other person is in the way.

13

Making the Most of Meetings

Why on earth do we spend so much of our work lives in meetings? Truth serum time: how many meetings did you attend today? This week? This month? Probably too many. So, how come we have so many meetings, taking up so much time, with so little progress? Are there any workarounds for improving your odds of gaining value from meetings? What can you do to work around meeting ineffectiveness and claw back some of your valuable time?

Here's a meeting assessment tool that you should apply to the meetings you have attended this week. If you were the meeting organizer, you can send this practical tool to your attendees. Ask the attendees to consider two large questions in answering each of the five items: (1) clarity of purpose, outcome, and actions for each area, and (2) perceived value relative to time spent.

Rate each of the five items that follow on a scale of 1 to 5.

1 means no value whatsoever—should have done something else

2 means some value but not really worth the time

3 means nothing special, nothing awful

4 means one of the better uses of my time

5 means absolutely valuable—one of the best things I could have done with my time

1. **Meeting purpose.** How clearly defined was the meeting purpose? How important was it from your perspective?

2. **Information sharing.** How valuable was the information to you in performing your job?

3. **Issue identification and problem solving.** How clearly defined were the problems or issues being addressed? How significant were those problems or issues from your perspective?

4. **Decision making.** Were important decisions made along with clearly defined responsibilities for carrying them out?

5. **Work planning and next actions.** Did the meeting end with clearly defined work plans, next actions, and due dates? How valuable were those outcomes compared with the time spent to get there?

Add up your total points, and multiply that number by 4. That result puts you in a context against 100 as a "perfect" score. Now think about your total score relative to earning letter grades in school. If you arrived at a total score of 60 (e.g., 5 items each with a rating of 3, multiplied by 4), then you have a more definite sense of how futile many meetings just may be. If you scored as high as 70, you're nevertheless stuck in C-level work. Getting to 80 would indicate just above B. If you got to 90 or higher, perhaps you should patent your meeting process!

If you're like most people, most of your meetings will fall well below 80.

That brings us to the 80/20 rule, sometimes referred to as the Pareto principle. A simplified definition is that roughly 80 percent of the effects come from 20 percent of the causes. Sales organizations often point to 80 percent of their sales coming from 20 percent of their customers. A process engineer once told me that 80 percent of the value obtained from a process typically comes from the first 20 percent of that process.

Could it be that 80 percent of your meeting value comes from just 20 percent of your meetings? Even more startling to contemplate, could 80 percent of any particular meeting's value come from just 20 percent of the meeting? It's certainly been true in my experience.

THE UPDATE DILEMMA

Often, meetings devolve into updates, in the form of either a senior manager updating those present or team members updating the leader. While updates are important, we all know those deadly round-robin meetings in which everyone gets a chance to update everyone else, boring one another to tears with endless Power-Point presentations.

To be fair, there are some circumstances under which updates and announcements are best delivered in a meeting format, but very few. Meetings can be appropriate when there is something dramatic to report, someone to acknowledge for an outstanding contribution, or an event in which surprise is part of the purpose.

There is a time and place for each of those assemblages, but plain old updates seem to suck the air out of the room as people sit there getting even further behind while work stacks up back at their desktops. Given the growing mounds of work that most of us face, it's no wonder people pop open laptops during meetings or run their thumbs raw keeping up with their BlackBerries.

Here's an example of someone who found a great solution to the need for meaningful updates, along with a great workaround to meeting mania. As you will see, the result benefited not just the group involved but a much wider base of employees in the organization as well.

Jim, a newly hired manager for a global provider of security and data-management services, had taken over a promising yet struggling division of the organization that provided solutions and support to 10,000 field staff. He had 34 direct reports spread around the globe. Keeping tabs on what everyone was doing, what progress people were making, and what issues they were encountering was the equivalent of a full-time job.

Staff meetings were a challenge, to say the least, with conflicts among time zones, travel schedules, customer meetings, and a host of other "normal" events preventing anything from being scheduled in a smooth and easy manner. When people did get together, meetings tended to follow the usual information update drill: some updates were useful to some attendees, but virtually nothing was important to all.

Jim's brainchild bears on many of the workaround challenges we are exploring across this book. He introduced a fresh approach to updates by requiring that each solution and product manager create a single-page summary of his or her accomplishments in the week just ended along with what the manager hoped to accomplish in the coming week. The department had four strategic performance objectives, and those four objectives served as the basic organizing construct for the weekly update—each objective had a line or two focused on the week gone by and a line or two dedicated to the coming week.

People quickly got with the program, generating these simple reports on a consistent basis. Several benefits began to surface. First of all, people avoided those long, drawn-out meeting updates! Second, by centering on the four strategic objectives, the reports served to reinforce what mattered most to the group. The reports also required all contributors to dedicate a few moments each week to reviewing their work from the higher perspective of intention and accountability (accomplishments and requirements) rather than the more familiar "busy-ness"—what I accomplished versus what I did.

Early on, people were encouraged to circulate their one-page updates to those in the company who would be impacted by the progress made. This initiative proved so valuable to those on the receiving end that the managers then took the added step of posting their updates to a central database so that anyone could track progress on critical projects and strategic objectives.

Today those updates are posted in a blog format so that anyone can easily surf posts chronologically as well as by project, objective, and business area. If Jim needed any additional validation about the value being created by this new and improved weekly update, it came when one of his reports was on vacation and did not post an update. Jim got several e-mail messages from people elsewhere in the company asking what happened—they had become reliant on those updates for their own planning purposes!

Not only had Jim produced a super workaround for meeting mania, but he also elicited indirect workarounds for potential performance gaps within his division. Using the succinct updates, he could identify hot spots as warning signs showed up and suggest responses, rather than waiting for them to blow up, and he could also spot areas where more coaching or training would be needed. Not bad for a simple weekly review!

CREATING VALUABLE MEETINGS

Back in 1986, Andrew Grove, the legendary founder and chairman of Intel, wrote a classic book, *High Output Management*. In the fourth chapter, "Meetings—the Medium of Management Work," he offered advice on how to get more out of meetings. He opened the chapter by writing:

> Meetings have a bad name. One school of management thought considers them the curse of the manager's existence. But there is another way to regard meetings . . . a meeting is nothing less than the medium through which managerial work is performed. That means we should not be fighting their very existence, but rather use the time spent in them as efficiently as possible.

Now, there's a thought: use your time in meetings efficiently and get your work done. What would efficient use of meeting time look like?

Grove proposed two types of meetings, and Intel moved straight down this path for years. The "process meeting" was a regularly scheduled event that managers were required to hold with their direct reports, and it came in three flavors: the one-on-one, the staff meeting, and the operations review. The "mission meeting" was usually held ad hoc and was designed to produce a specific output, frequently a decision.

It's been 25 years since this advice came out, and much of it still holds today. To bring the advice even more up to date, it may be helpful to amend Grove's breakdown of the two meeting types. Staff meetings and operations reviews have a tendency to revert to flaccid updates, with each participant straining to appear relevant. If we leave updates to another form or forum, we may then arrive at two basic meeting types, each with different purposes and outcomes. Both are versions of Grove's mission meeting:

1. The issue identification and resolution meeting

   a. What's in the way?

   b. Why does it matter (impact, risk, etc.)?

   c. What's it costing us?

   d. How could we move forward?

   e. What help is needed?

2. The decision-making meeting

   a. What kind of decision needs to be made?

   b. Who will be impacted by it?

   c. Who has what kind of decision rights for this particular issue?

      • Who has the right to be consulted prior to the decision?

      • Who has the right to be informed after the decision is made?

      • Who has the right to make the final decision?

The issue resolution meeting utilizes those present to help identify barriers and solutions. When calling this type of meeting, the meeting organizer should identify the issues to be addressed in the meeting invitation and specify the kind of help needed to move the issue forward.

If you get invited to an issue resolution meeting without a clear purpose or agenda, it is fair game to ask what the organizer hopes to gain by your presence. That way, you can beg off when you have nothing of significance to contribute. Likewise, if there is an important role for you or contribution you can make, then you can better prepare for the meeting and the value expected.

Similarly, when it comes to decision meetings, the organizer should consider what input he or she needs, from whom, and why. Some people in the organization should be consulted before a decision is made because of their experience and expertise or because of the potential impact on their areas of responsibility. If you need to do some consultation before making a decision, consider whether a group meeting is the best forum or if you would be better served with one-to-one meetings.

These two meeting types become workarounds that work by reducing the number of meetings people must attend as well as the number of people who need to meet. By clarifying the difference between idea generation and actual decision making, you can avoid having the wrong people in a meeting, you can shorten the amount of time each meeting requires, and you can even eliminate some meetings altogether.

General Guidelines for Effective Meetings

When planning a meeting, there are a few guidelines that can help you deliver something people will consider a good use of their time. As always, start with purpose and intention. Why are people meeting? What outcome are you intending to produce? What role or contribution do you expect from those attending? Make certain you communicate purpose, outcome, and contribution to those you invite.

Common purposes for which meeting in person or by teleconference may make sense include generating ideas concerning a specific issue or opportunity, identifying roadblocks or risks associated with key goals or projects, brainstorming solutions to those roadblocks or risks, and contributing to a decision process.

Agendas that spell out the purpose and outcome you are targeting will help people prepare, but only if sent early enough to allow time for preparation. Include a specific statement about your intended outcome for each agenda item. The agenda should also include any supporting materials necessary (briefing documents, background material, data, etc.). If the only purpose of the meeting is general updates, then consider other alternatives such as e-mail or database postings.

One of the symptoms of meeting madness is the lack of clarity around purpose. Some people may attend thinking they are supposed to be pushing toward a decision, while others may be slowing things down because they think the purpose is to examine options, uncover risk, and otherwise analyze the situation. Picture a meeting in which two fairly senior folks are singing from different song sheets: one is driving hard for a decision, while the other is constantly offering up new ideas. Neither can understand what possesses the other. Think there might be some potential for a few sparks to fly?

Here are some ideas and tips that should help you through every step of the meeting, from before it starts to after it's finished:

Before the Meeting

1. If it's your meeting, provide sufficient briefing materials so that participants can arrive prepared. Let the participants know that you expect them to arrive prepared.

2. When invited to a meeting, ask for details on the purpose, the intended outcome, and the role you are expected to play if these matters are not clear in the invitation. Be sure you know what value the meeting organizer would like to gain from your participation.

3. If you are being invited only to provide an update on something, ask if an e-mail or some other briefing document would suffice.

It's important to make sure that only the right people for the meeting show up to it. The decision maker doesn't need to sit through the brainstorming session that creates the decision options. However, if you're actually trying to decide something or solve a particular problem, you better make certain the decision authority is in the room!

If you are simply consulting with people, soliciting input and points of view, restrict attendance to those who should have input either by dint of their experience or because their role allows them the right to provide input. If, on the other hand, you are making an actual decision, invite only those whose input you need to validate or implement the decision.

During the Meeting

1. If you are attending a meeting, and the purpose, outcome, and expected contributions have not been made clear, ask the meeting organizer if you can take five minutes to clarify before diving into the agenda.

2. If you are attending or organizing a meeting, whether in person, by conference call, or by videoconference, be sure to do the following:

   a. Introduce or clarify who is attending and their roles.

   b. Establish ground rules for acceptable behavior: for example, no processing e-mail, no use of BlackBerries, no outside calls, iPhones off.

   c. Be mindful of particular room noises, casual jokes, or details of visual presentations that may not be obvious to those attending remotely.

   d. Regularly ask for input from remote attendees; consider asking remote participants to lead one or more agenda items, or to kick off brainstorming or idea-generation sessions, so they feel included and not overwhelmed by those in the main conference room.

3. Arrive briefed and ready to contribute in the role or roles for which you have been asked to participate.

4. Always ask for specific action steps following each agenda item, and clarify who has responsibility for them and when you or the team should expect completion of each step.

After the Meeting

1. Conclude each meeting with a short (less than five-minute) evaluation process on the meeting's value:

   a. Meeting purpose

   b. Information sharing

   c. Issue identification and problem solving

   d. Decision making

   e. Work planning and next actions

OBSTACLES TO MEETING EFFICIENCY

In certain meetings, you may need all of the team present in order to validate a decision and/or to receive new marching orders, especially if the decision is likely to generate new action plans. The larger the group attending any one meeting, the more likely you are to encounter people embodying two common roadblocks: lack of preparation and being disengaged. Both can be dealt with.

Work Around the Unprepared Participant

One of my clients in the aerospace industry complained that update meetings would often devolve into oral briefings for those attending, rather than digging into the more substantive issues they were facing and how to resolve them quickly. Frequently, meetings needed to be rescheduled once everyone was on the same page because those who had been briefed then needed time to digest the information. This need to meet and meet again was producing enormous schedule delays, and at the tune of $1 million a day, delays had a way of being significant.

From experience, the program manager knew that these kinds of repetitive meetings were commonplace in the industry, and he thought up a solution that required a bit of chutzpah. He sent out a briefing document for his first substantive schedule-review meeting accompanied by a note stating that there would be a short quiz on the briefing document before the formal meeting began. The note explained that those passing the quiz would be entitled to full participation rights in the meeting; those failing the quiz would be relegated to observer status only—they would not be allowed to speak! Like I said, chutzpah! Risky too, you might think. After all, these are rocket scientists!

The first meeting produced 100 percent success in terms of all participants passing the quiz. From then on, the quiz became a meeting standard. People loved the "pressure," teased one another about being ready, and enjoyed the slightly competitive nature of being tested. The net result was that they cut meeting times substantially while reducing the total number of meetings required by half. Not only did arriving prepared, knowledgeable, and ready to go reduce meeting time, but also the group reduced the time to complete the mission from a budget of 54 months to 27 months.

Obviously, not all of the success in reducing the schedule can be attributed to a quiz, but the quiz did get people on the same page, more efficiently involved, and actively looking for other available workarounds. My guess is that everyone has suffered through meetings with the unprepared participant. What would happen if you shared this novel idea with your team members? With your boss?

Work Around the Disengaged Participant

How many meetings have you attended in which participants were more disengaged than engaged? You see people with laptops open, processing e-mail or working on project deliverables, not to mention the furious thumbing of the CrackBerry addicted, or those who pop out for those oh-so-important calls. Why do people even bother to turn up if they're not really there to participate?

The answers to that rhetorical question could lie in politics and culture as easily as in the fear that something important might actually surface. My general observations over the years would suggest that very few people find meetings valuable, and so e-mail, BlackBerries, and iPhones give them the opportunity to at least get something done.

If your meetings are populated by players who are disengaged, take heart. Here are a few suggestions that have proved effective:

1. Start with your intended purpose and outcomes; solicit agreement that these are worth pursuing, and confirm that those attending have reason to participate. If someone begs off due to lack of interest or business context, allow him or her to leave, and then make certain that for future meetings the right people are invited.

2. Establish a ground rule that laptops and wireless devices are to remain closed except for reference or note taking.

3. Clarify participation guidelines—no cell phones or outside calls. Ask if anyone has any fires or crises looming or conflicting calls or meetings, and plan accordingly.

4. Assign response-ability, in advance, for each agenda item to different participants.

5. If you still have distracted or disengaged attendees, consider calling a break and taking the individual aside to find out if something is distracting him or her—there could be a valid reason! If someone is just not that interested, you can always

invite the person to leave and get on with whatever it is that is more important. After the meeting, you can circle back and ask if the individual still needs to be on the meeting invite list. Be careful here—this workaround requires well-chosen words and a light touch!

MEETING ALTERNATIVES

If you are swamped with meetings, here are a few options that may work for you.

Use Video- or Teleconferencing

Technology can streamline the meeting process when effectively applied, or it can become just another time waster. That's why it's important that you don't just employ technology arbitrarily.

- On the upside, video- or teleconferencing can be an effective workaround for meetings of marginal value and certainly can minimize other disruptions such as long-distance travel or even just the time it takes to cross from one building to the next.

- On the downside, many people have learned that they can utilize the teleconference facility to functionally avoid the meeting while still being nominally present.

- Be wary of "participants" who use meetings to multitask—doing e-mail, stepping out for other calls, or performing other kinds of work while the meeting is in process. If you need someone to be in the room, make certain the person is actually "in the room," not lost in e-mail land or in transit between other tasks.

- If you are required to attend meetings with little or no apparent value, the teleconference could be a built-in workaround that enables you to get more work done by avoiding having to convene in the conference room.

In 90 percent of the meetings I see in larger organizations, a goodly number of people attend by telephone, primarily due to the geographic spread of key players. Well-intentioned and theoretically useful applications of teleconferencing can still waste time and talent by not employing effective meeting protocols.

Rules for Effective Teleconferencing

- Make sure everybody knows who is on the phone, introducing everybody and polling locations for participants.

- Be considerate of those phoning in. Often, the host team is in a single conference room, and the conversation tends to become dominated by those in the room. Simple and obvious things can kill the meeting for those phoning in, such as insider jokes and people talking over one another. It's easy to figure out what's going on if you are in the room, but it can be hard if you're on the phone. If you aren't considerate of those on the phone, you may be encouraging them to multi-task. I've even witnessed a participant with his phone on mute while holding another, unrelated meeting in person, just because the teleconference was so useless!

- If you're brainstorming or moving toward a decision, the leader needs to make a conscious effort to poll those attending by telephone, asking pointed questions to engage them and periodically summarizing findings, conclusions, or specific decisions.

Replace Weekly Staff Meetings with Weekly Review Meetings

Instead of conducting the usual round-robin, activity-based updates, with or without PowerPoint detailing the activities and the "I said, they said" blow-by-blows, consider gearing staff meetings to *accomplishments* and *support needed* to accomplish even more next week.

The process might include the following key components:

- What I accomplished (milestones, deliverables, projects completed, etc.)

- What I did not do and why (what got in the way—think control and influence)

- Where I need assistance

  - Training or resource required

  - Leadership air cover to influence another group, team, or department

  - Management support in removing barriers or creating new workarounds

- What's coming next week—major milestones or deliverables

  - Any help needed?

  - Any danger of slippage?

Replace Weekly Review Meetings with Weekly Review Blogs

Even though weekly review meetings are a big upgrade over traditional staff meetings, they are meetings nonetheless and require people to convene in one form or another. It can pay to explore the idea of replacing the weekly review meeting with weekly-review blog posts to an internal site. This option can be especially attractive if the team is located in multiple geographic areas and time zones. The information is still available, but it is delivered at a considerable savings of both time and logistical juggling.

- Restrict weekly-review blogs to single-page updates.

  - What I accomplished in the last seven days

  - What I plan to accomplish in the next seven days

  - How each accomplishment links to key goals, objectives, and projects

- E-mail the blog or database links to impacted parties until this approach becomes your standard updating procedure.

Update on the Fly

If the occasional update is necessary, why not do the update on the fly? For example, could you walk to the cafeteria with a coworker, your boss, or your direct reports and update while on the way for a cup of coffee? If you need to meet in an office, a slightly twisted idea is to meet while standing—no chairs allowed. As soon as we settle in, we inevitably settle down for that "long winter's night."

Meetings suck up time—we all know that. Some are purely pointless, while others may have value. One common denominator is that they consume time and require scheduling gymnastics. If you can accomplish the result by some form of electronic updating (e-mail, database, blog post, etc.), you may achieve the storied win-win: everyone gets the information needed while saving time in the process. If getting together still seems necessary, then do consider various forms of teleconferencing—just be sure to incorporate the protocols that help maintain course and facilitate contributions from those calling in.

WORKAROUND QUESTIONS

Meeting workarounds can be awfully tricky primarily because they involve multiple other people. Those other people could include your boss, other higher-ups, and people from other teams, all against the backdrop of politics in general. When you're looking for workaround options, here are some questions that may help you determine whether meeting is necessary and, if so, in what format:

1. Are there specific accomplishments, milestones, or deliverables that need to be reviewed?

   - Was anything accomplished for which some form of acknowledgment, recognition, or even celebration would be valuable?

- Are there lessons learned that would be valuable to share with the larger team? (Sometimes meetings are the best format if teaching is an outcome; otherwise, lean toward database or blog posts to track lessons.)

2. Are there notable milestones, objectives, or deliverables expected in the next week or two?

   - Anything in jeopardy for which creative planning or contribution from team members will be helpful?

   - Any areas in which one or more of the team members may need assistance?

3. Do you have a big announcement looming for which in-person meetings may be the best way to deliver the news?

   - A big contract awarded?

   - Change in strategic direction?

   - Introduction of new players?

4. Could the purpose and outcome of the meeting be accomplished in another format or venue?

   - Teleconference?

   - Weekly review via e-mail, database, or blog-type posting?

14

The E-Mail Avalanche

The sales manager of an apparel company had more than 600 unopened e-mail messages in his in-box, ranging in age from a few hours to more than two weeks. The senior VP of a major technology company had more than 3,000 e-mail messages in his in-box, hundreds of which had not been read. The program manager for an aerospace company averaged 200 new messages a day. E-mail is a marvelous conceptual tool, but it has also become a nightmare on many levels, mainly in the visage of the exploding volume of messages and the phenomenon of out of sight, out of mind, that comes with a bursting, out-of-control in-box.

Here are a few questions for you to scan as you get ready to trek through your own version of the e-mail avalanche:

- How many messages do you have in your in-box right now?

- How many of those messages have you opened at least once?

- What do you do with the e-mail once you have read it?

- How much e-mail do you receive in an average day?

- How much of that e-mail do you actually need to see?

- How much e-mail do you receive with the infamous heading "FYI"?

- Have you sent a message to someone and are still waiting to hear back from the recipient?

- Has someone sent you a message and is waiting for your response in turn?

- How do you keep track of all the responses you are waiting for or need to send?

There are numerous challenges presented by e-mail, many of which require some kind of workaround or another. E-mail workarounds are made even more challenging by the fact that each person with whom you communicate electronically is likely to treat e-mail differently from how you treat it, and neither of you may know what the other considers appropriate.

Some people watch their in-boxes all day long and respond as soon as something shows up; some organizational cultures even seem to demand instant response. Other people are content to check their in-boxes once or twice a day. As hard as it may be to believe, some look at their e-mail only once or twice a week!

Many people allow their e-mail in-boxes to grow and grow, often reading a message, not being sure what to do with it, and calmly moving on to the next one. And if they're not clear about what to do with that one, they will close it and open the next. At this rate, it's not hard to clog up an in-box. If this sounds uncomfortably like your in-box, then you may be creating at least two levels of "stuckness": one level impacting your own work, and another level impacting others ranging from team members and other parts of the organization to customers, suppliers, or other outside parties.

As is ever the case with workarounds, you may need to break the issues down into two broad categories: those caused by others and those caused by your own practices.

INFORMATION OVERLOAD

Two corporations were codeveloping a highly technical product and were encountering serious delays. I was asked to take a look at how they were managing the joint development effort to see if I had any advice on what they could do to accelerate the process. Normally, I see organizations slowing each other down in disagreements about who should lead which part of the effort, who has the better design or testing process, who has better quality control, and so forth. I'm sure you have seen something like this yourself.

This time, I discovered two partners working in one of the more highly collaborative fashions I had ever seen. They shared everything. As in *everything*. If you have ever heard the cliché that a strength overused becomes a weakness, here was the poster child. Both teams had seen previous efforts run aground because information had not been freely shared with the other team. They had therefore agreed that they would not allow information blockades on this project. Whenever people had any kind of new information, they tended to share it with everyone via e-mail. That included everything from ordinary status updates and data from testing to design changes and quality deficiencies. Some people put everyone in the "To" line, while others put most people in the "Cc" line, further adding to the confusion about who was expected to respond. While admirable in its intent to maintain "transparency," the practice summarily clogged just about everyone's e-mail in-box.

Most team members wound up spending two to three hours a day reading e-mail messages from one another. As soon as I pointed this out to the joint project team, the leader bristled, complaining that I couldn't have it both ways—it's not fair to be scolded for sharing too much information while simultaneously being scolded for not sharing enough. Much of what moves around e-mail these days is generally classified as information. However, we all could probably benefit from a better definition of information if we are going to streamline the process of disseminating it. As soon as I helped the teams to redefine the term in a more useful manner, e-mail traffic dropped nearly 70 percent!

Workaround: Is It Really Information?

How could redefining information turn into a workaround? I will show you by using a method employed previously in this book. *Information* is a word made up of several words. As mentioned in Chapter 5 while discussing communication, any word with the suffix *ation*, as well as any variant that ends with *tion* or *ion*, generally means "requires action." Quite a variety of words contain that suffix, and they indicate that action is required. If you combine *inform* with *action*, you produce a word that means something akin to "inform for action." Information, then, should inform someone on some aspect of action required.

Now let's return to the team members who were struggling with information overload. Each of them had been getting deluged with FYI kinds of messages, many of which were periodic updates that required no action whatsoever. General updates did need to be tracked and archived, but most people on the e-mail chain had no real need to be updated as frequently as they were.

I suggested that the team members reroute e-mail traffic by agreeing to file updates directly to their project database. However, someone wisely pointed out that buried inside some updates were specific actions that needed to be taken or requests for further information from one or more of the recipients. The team leader quickly got the point: if it's just a general update, then it belongs in the update archive, to which everyone had access. If, however, the update also included a request for specific action, follow-up, or additional information, it needed to go to the specific individuals or subordinate teams with specific, clear requests for whatever action was needed.

Making that simple little differentiation trimmed large distribution lists down to small, relevant lists of recipients. The team eventually agreed that project updates would be generated on specific days of the week and would be placed directly into the archives. Someone who needed to read an update knew where to go and when in order to receive it. To better enable those involved to determine if the update needed to go to the archive or to a distribution list, I helped them compile a set of questions to ask themselves before hitting the Send button:

1. Who needs to know this?

2. Why do they need to know?

3. What action do we expect them to take?

4. Within what time parameters do we need the response?

5. Are there other contingencies that need to be considered?

6. Who else needs the output of the action?

That set of questions helped them cut down on traffic considerably.

Next, the team members worked to define protocols both for addressing e-mail and for replying. They agreed that if something required action from a person or team, those were the names that would go in the "To" field. As much as they liked the archive idea, they still wanted people to know that an update had been generated. That led to using the "Cc" line for people who might need to know but from whom no specific action was required. People soon learned that if they were in the "To" line, they needed to read carefully because an action or response was expected. Those in the "Cc" line knew they could simply skim and then delete; they were up to date.

However, people wrote updates in all kinds of ways; some were short and concise, and some were encyclopedic in their style and documentation. That made for some head scratching in determining what kind of action someone might need to take. With a little prodding from me, the team members looked into e-mail etiquette and arrived at a set of rules they would find useful. Between our internal discussions and some Internet surfing, the team leader settled on the protocols reproduced here, which were then distributed to the entire program team.

E-Mail Etiquette

Tired of spending too much time sifting through e-mail? Be part of the solution rather than part of the problem. Take the time to digest the following advice and help make everyone's day a little easier:

- Ask yourself, "Who really needs to see this?" More often than not, not everyone needs to know. Use "Cc" and Reply to All sparingly. When using Reply to All, remove all names no longer relevant to the e-mail.

- Before using Reply to All, scan the address list and the full content of the e-mail to ensure that something intended for specific individuals does not go to outside entities.

- When copying people (or using Reply to All), explain how the message pertains to each person. If several people need to see it, call out each recipient or group by assigning actions or providing information on why each was included. For example:

  - Jack: Decision needed. Get marketing to approve the draft.

  - Natalie: Please verify. Does the title capture our message?

  - Ed, Frank, Willy: FYI. If we need a redesign, you might expect a delay.

- Ensure that the "Subject" line accurately names the topic. Minor topic changes should be made at the end of the title, for searchability. If a topic changes totally, change the title. This makes it easier for readers to scan their mailboxes and determine which messages are most important and what actions they have to take. (For example, instead of just "Deadline," use "Action: Need your input by May 5.")

- When forwarding long threads, give your reader context. Don't force recipients to read through the whole chain to understand what action is required of them. Take time to edit the forwarded messages. Give them only what is relevant, and be clear on how it pertains.

- Keep messages succinct and to the point. If the subject requires more than what fits on a person's screen (without scrolling), perhaps a conversation (by phone or face-to-face) would be a better method of conveying your message.

- Make action requests clear. Often, action requests require some explanation and background. That's fine, but highlight what action is required of the recipient by placing it at the beginning. If the e-mail is addressed to more than one person, be explicit about who needs to do what.

- Ask yourself, "Is e-mail the best way to communicate this message?" If it's to a single person, especially complex, especially sensitive, or time critical, using the phone or speaking face-to-face may be more effective and less time-consuming. We are colocated for a reason.

- Be prudent with your use of attachments. Be mindful of BlackBerry or other "smartphones" users and, if practical, both attach your file and paste its text into the body of the e-mail. Try to avoid sending attachments larger than 5 MB. Instead, post your file in an eRoom or other form of database and send a link.

- Limit the use of the "Important" flag to when it's really necessary. This will preserve the effectiveness of this tool for when you really need the recipient to drop everything and take immediate action.

REDUCING THE FREQUENCY OF E-MAIL CHECKING

Tony Schwartz, author of a new bestseller, *The Way We're Working Isn't Working,* offers another piece of useful advice for managing both your e-mail and your time. He told me about working with one of his clients, a large consulting firm. Twelve- to 14- hour days were the norm, and e-mail played a large role in people's working so long.

One young partner was virtually wedded to his e-mail program, constantly stopping what he was doing whenever the pinging alerted him that another new message had arrived. As a former associate partner at Andersen Consulting (Accenture), I know well the drill of overwhelming volumes of e-mail and the expectation of immediate response.

On Tony's advice, the young partner moved from always-checking-instantly-replying mode to checking e-mail just twice a day, once at 10:15 A.M. and again at 2:30 P.M. Before switching to this schedule, he could hardly keep up with the volume. Afterward, he found he could get back to zero messages in his in-box twice a day. Part of the underlying rationale was that by turning his attention twice a day to his e-mail, he not only freed himself from constant interruptions but also was able to focus better when he was handling his messages.

However, before this approach could work, he had to reset expectations from his fellow partners and coworkers. He did so by letting everyone know his e-mail protocols and also told everyone that if something urgent arose, all the person had to do was ping him by cell phone, which he promised to answer no matter what. Nine months after instituting this practice, he had yet to receive one such urgent call!

One simple way to implement your own version of this switch is to include your new protocol as part of your signature line. Let people know your e-mail processing standards, and set specified response intervals. For example:

- I reply within 24 hours—let me know if you need a response more urgently.

- I read and reply to e-mail three times a day: 8:00 A.M., 1:00 P.M., and 4:00 P.M.

- If this requires an urgent response, please call my cell phone at 123-555-5555.

Out of Sight, Out of Mind

You may be on the receiving end of 100 to 300 incoming messages that land on your screen each day. Furthermore, as well as being the recipient, you may be generating volume yourself. Often, volume grows because somebody sent a message to one person and then cc'd a dozen others. That can lead to a dozen or more Reply to All messages, ranging from something additive to versions of "Huh? Why am I getting this?"

Regardless of how many messages come in on any given day, many of us open messages, find we aren't sure what to do, and simply move to the next one. That can turn an in-box into a memory device of some kind, under the assumption that as long as it's in the in-box, it can be retrieved if necessary.

I suppose that's true at one level, but an in-box is best utilized as a place for new messages, not items you have already seen. Here are three golden rules for handling an incoming message efficiently:

- Clarify what it is (information, action request, response request, etc.).

- Determine what action is required.

- Take the action now or have a means of tracking it for action later (to-do list, calendar, action folder, etc.).

In short, letting it stay buried in the in-box is not the best solution.

Depending on the screen dimensions, e-mail provider, and font size, you are likely to see 20 to 30 e-mail entries at any one time. That's fine if you have no more than 20 to 30, but what happens if you have several hundred? Or more? Most people with hundreds or even thousands of e-mail messages stuffed in their in-boxes manage to work through only a couple of screens of messages a day, with the most recent arrivals on top. If something important lands in the in-box and you don't have time to clarify what it is and what to do about it, it can easily keep dropping down the queue until "out of sight, out of mind" becomes the de facto reality of your system.

That can create significant risk, both to you and to others who may be depending on you for input, advice, action, or approval.

Workaround: Unclog Your In-Box

The most effective thing you can do if you suffer from a clogged, out-of-control in-box is to move everything that is older than a month over to an archive folder. You could label this folder "Didn't Know What to Do" or anything you prefer. Just get those messages out of your in-box. A month is an arbitrary limit and should be adjusted to suit your situation. If something has been there for a month and someone really needed you to respond, the sender might well have sent you another message anyway. If the message is just for your reference, filing it in an archive folder will allow you to search for it if the need arises.

Now what do you do with the slightly smaller stack that's left? One at a time, open the items and ask three simple questions: (1) What is this? (2) Is it actionable? (3) If so, what action is required? There are more sophisticated questions that can go into this process, but these three will get you going. If you can answer the first question, you should also have an idea about whether the message matters and why. If you can't answer the first or second questions, you can either return the message to the sender and ask why it was sent to you or move it over to that archive folder.

If it is not actionable now, you should question why you need it. It could be reference material, data, or some other kind of information that you will need to access later. If this is the case, it goes in a reference folder if you may need it for supporting information later, or in a tickler file if you need to be reminded sometime downstream. If it's not reference or for action later, it may just be something that can be deleted.

If it is actionable, then you are down to three choices:

- **Do it now.** Best practice suggests that if you can do whatever it is in two minutes or less, there likely isn't anything better, faster, or more efficient that you could do, so just do it!

- **Delegate it.** If it needs to be done, and it requires more than two minutes, ask yourself if the task requires you personally to act or if you could delegate it to someone. If you can delegate it, then forward the message right now along with instructions about what you want to be done and when.

- **Defer it.** It could be that you need to do it yourself but not right now. If that's the case, you can add it to one of two basic reminder locations: your task or to-do list or a calendar page. Once you have it stored in a system that will remind you that it needs action, you can do one of three things with the e-mail. You could either delete it, file it in an "Action Required" folder with a cross-reference to your task or to-do list, or save it in a reference folder if you think you may need to access it later.

By plowing through your in-box in this manner, you have much to gain:

- You should get a whole lot of things unstuck and moving again.

- You may catch a few things that were in danger of erupting into one of those fires and crises we discussed in Chapter 11.

- You will get current and back in control!

Once you have cleaned up your in-box in this fashion, all you need to do is process incoming e-mail once or twice a day, following the same basic protocol, and you will be able to *stay* current and in control. Worst case, make this process part of your weekly review as also outlined in Chapter 11, so that when you leave on Friday, your in-box is back to zero. That doesn't mean everyone else will be current and in control; however, *you* will be. If you recall the control-influence-respond model from the first chapter, you may now be in an ideal position to influence others and help guide them on the way to getting current and in control as well.

TEACHING OTHERS E-MAIL EFFICIENCY

If you were to Google "e-mail etiquette" today, you would find 46,300,000 entries. I guess e-mail behavior is a hot button that more than a few have noticed. Plenty of dos and don'ts probably come to mind when you think about e-mail etiquette, including such standbys as don't shout in ALL CAPS, don't forward hoaxes, restrict your jokes to your close friends, and keep your antivirus program up to date. Taking a broader look, what you really need is to help others gain some efficiency themselves. Drains on efficiency commonly occur because of one or more of the following:

- Lack of clarity about what the sender wants or needs

- Lack of clarity on the recipient's part about what action to take

- FYI messages with no inform-for-action in them

- Reply to All

- Conflation of the "To" and "Cc" lines

- Out of sight, out of mind

- Lack of context for timeliness—when is the response or action needed?

You might have cleaned up your e-mail in-box and adopted sensible, efficient practices on your side of the equation, but what can you do if others aren't quite up to the same standards? Besides leveraging the ideas mentioned earlier, here are a few tips that you may need to employ. There's no question that to make these work, you will have to engage in even more steps, but the extra effort may prove worthwhile if it really matters that you receive timely responses.

First and foremost, the game involves making it easy on the other guy. The basics are still in play: be sure that the "Subject" line tells recipients what you want, and start each message with a clear explanation of purpose, action requested, and appropriate supporting information, which Sally McGhee advises in her book *Take Back Your Life*. Sally also offers advice on how you use the "Subject" line to help. I have combined some of her recommendations with others I have found valuable.

Use the "Subject" line for clarity on what you are asking the recipient to do. You may want to develop a shorthand that you can use first within your own group, perhaps eventually migrating to others in the organization. Here's an example:

AR: Action required—recipient needs to do something specific

RR: Response required—you need the recipient's input, point of view, permission, or the like

RO: Read only

BD: Briefing document enclosed for meeting on [date]

SU: Status update

FYI: And it better be something the person needs to know!

EOM: End of message

Use the "To" line for people who need to act on the message.

Use the "Cc" line for people who need to know about the action but do not have to take action themselves.

Never reply to all—reply only to those who need to know what you are writing about or need to act on the content of your message.

Always change the "Subject" line to reflect what you're doing. For example:

Confirming receipt of Project X update message

Confirming appointment request

Taking action on Project Y per your request

Need more information regarding Project Z

From there, you may need to take a few extra steps to make certain the message is actually read and appropriate action is taken. For example, if you know that the other person is habitually slow in getting around to messages, for whatever the reason, then consider one or more of the following:

- Leave a voice message letting the person know the e-mail is there, what it's about, what you need, and by when.

- Leave a text message letting the person know the e-mail is there, what it's about, what you need, and by when.

- Knock on the person's door or cube and let him or her know you sent an e-mail requiring response or action.

- Print the e-mail and leave it on the person's chair.

To help you keep track of what you are waiting for, try the following:

- Send a copy of the e-mail to yourself and track it on a Waiting for Reply list or in an e-mail folder.

- Send a copy to yourself and enter it on your calendar for follow-up.

- Review your Waiting for Reply list or e-mail folder at least once a week, and follow up with the person if you haven't heard back. Make this part of your weekly review.

If you want to work around the e-mail avalanche, then you will need to cover two different areas. In a nutshell, the solution to the e-mail avalanche is one part self-workaround and one part system or other people workarounds.

The overall message here is that you have a lot to do in your job and precious little time to do it. The more you can cut down on e-mail traffic, the better off you will be. Eliminating the need to keep rereading messages stored in your in-box will enhance your ability to get work done.

WORKAROUND QUESTIONS

Here are some workaround questions to help you dispatch snow-banks of e-mail:

1. Do you have any messages stored in your in-box that are simply there as reminders of work you need to perform? If so, move those reminders to a task list and either delete the e-mail message or store it in a reference folder on your system.

2. Do you have any messages for which you are unclear about the action required? If so, consult with the originator about the intended purpose, desired outcome, and required action.

3. Do you have a clearly established response protocol so people know when to expect replies from you? If not, consider establishing something, and include it in your signature line.

4. Does your team, work group, or department have its own e-mail protocols? If not, consider using tips provided in this chapter to spark a discussion on the subject so you can arrive at something that will help everyone. Be sure to cover some basics:

   • What constitutes information? Do updates belong in e-mail, or is there a better system for circulating and storing them?

   • How will everybody involved flag specific action requests in e-mail messages?

   • What standards should be adopted regarding expected replies?

   • When is Reply to All appropriate?

   • What is the difference in being named in the "To" line versus the "Cc" line? What expectations apply to which line regarding what the recipient should do?

5. Are you frequently copied on e-mail messages that do not apply to you? If so, either or both of the following actions could bring relief:

   • Reply to anyone sending you these messages with a request that you be taken off future e-mail strings unless specific action is being requested of you.

   • Send the originator a suggested protocol for how to address messages to distinguish between general information and specific requests for action.

15

When Process Gets in the Way

For many people, it seems as though process has become a dirty word, something to be avoided at all costs. The technology security and electronic medical records companies I mentioned in the opening chapter are prime examples. In both companies, experienced executives could see the need for process improvement in order to achieve efficiencies, but they were also fearful of binding the organization and stifling creativity. Some of the most experienced managers in these two companies had escaped overly bureaucratic and process-intensive organizations that had limited both creativity and initiative, and they had no intention of bringing that kind of restrictive thinking to their cool, fast-moving companies.

We have probably all experienced bureaucratic processes that seem somewhere between mindless and useless. The example from Chapter 2 about the state of California enforcing obsolete practices and out-of-date laws would seem to represent in spades what these executives fear. Who wants to take on the burden of repetitive processes that have outlived their usefulness?

Sometimes processes or other organizational rules need to be reengineered or set aside altogether. I remember meeting a lovely gentleman who owned a couple of black cabs in London. One day while driving me to Heathrow, Harry told me that English law still requires cabbies to carry a bale of hay in the boot, and they do not have to accept fares longer than six miles. Why? Because you just can't overwork that horse with such long fares, and you do need to stop and feed the poor bugger every once in a while. Cute, I suppose. Obviously, no one bothers with enforcing any regulation that blatantly outdated, but this example harks back to our earlier discourse about start, stop, and continue. Let's agree that six-mile fare restrictions and bales of hay belong in the "stop" bucket.

On either side of the ocean, what happens when you encounter burdensome processes that serve only to impede progress? What if the process actually works against its intended purpose? Again, it is important to think about original intent and keep in mind that the process you now find burdensome probably served a useful purpose at some point. The compliance process of the state of California had its roots in prudent financial-management practices. It just needed to be updated. Care and feeding of your horses makes sense as well, but we'd be safe to scrap that one from the procedures for modern-day taxi fleets.

Following are a pair of rich examples of processes that hindered and two very different workarounds.

THE IRREVERENT (BUT EFFECTIVE) MUSICIAN

This is one of the riskier versions of seeking forgiveness rather than approval. If you wish to implement anything this bold in your own job, you will need to be extremely confident in the outcome, as well as extremely willing to bear the wrath of potentially unforgiving managers. Make certain your résumé is current if you want to follow a similar path!

Evan Taubenfeld is a 25-year-old guitarist and instrumentalist who is flat-out not willing to let process get in the way of success—even if it is a "tried-and-true" process that has withstood "the test of time." In fact, Evan could be the spokesperson for challenging conventional wisdom. After several years of playing and writing music for other groups, he broke out with his debut solo album in May 2010. He says of himself:

> For the first time in my career, I'm not hiding behind anyone else, whether it be as a guitarist or drummer in someone else's band, or being the writer and producer. I've been sitting on the sidelines waiting for this for so long. I'm like that kid on the basketball team who is pretty good but rides the bench the entire season for three years until finally, the coach is like, "You're in. Don't screw this up." It's Chapter One of the story of my life.

I caught up with Evan on a particularly cool day, one that was revealing of both the kind of determination (intention, responseability, and commitment) he embodies and the kind of playful irreverence that has enabled him to continue climbing to the top of his musical genre.

Evan, under contract to Warner Music, put it this way: "Workarounds are the day-to-day life experience for a single entity tied to a large, bureaucratic record label." As irreverent as that may sound, he went on to display a level of wisdom and insight most of us would cherish.

He noted that there are important interests driving large record labels, and they are perfectly understandable. He also understands that while these companies might have developed a number of processes over the years that used to create value, some of those processes just don't work well with the current music scene and the way younger music fans find and buy music.

As he said, "These guys have some incredible strengths. The only problem is that sometimes those strengths turn into their greatest obstacles." Evan is on a mission to loosen up the industry so it can thrive in the next iteration of music supply and demand, as well as to have fun making music and getting it out to his fans. He is well aware of the differing interests between those on the front lines and those who work on the back end. The artists, the music scouts from various record labels who troll clubs every evening looking for talent, and the music fans are all about getting the right music out as fast as possible, while the VPs of marketing, sales, and distribution are all about following those "tried-and-true" processes that got them where they are now.

Here's a related example of how misalignment produces conflict:

Let's flip the calendar back to December 2009. Evan dashed off what he thought was a funny song that referenced country-music star Taylor Swift, naming the tune "Merry Swiftmas (Even Though I Celebrate Chanukah)." It's a playful song to Santa asking if the singer could have Taylor Swift for Christmas. He wrote the song and recorded it in a day. For the heck of it, he put it up on YouTube on December 7, with a still shot instead of a video, and tweeted the song to Taylor Swift, who responded, "This made me smile."

Well, it made a lot of their fans smile as well, capturing tens of thousands of views in just a couple of hours. Evan thought this was pretty cool, and even though his contract did not permit him to even post the song as he had, he then went on to create a music video the next day and posted that as well. The Internet went nuts, with more than 500,000 people watching the video and hearing the song. No two ways about it, this song resonated with a whole bunch of people. Thousands of requests came pouring in from fans asking where they could buy it. All this in two days.

Evan contacted his folks at Warner, asking that they release the song immediately on iTunes. They weren't exactly pleased. It hadn't gone through the "tried-and-true" process. No one had tested it for market acceptance or otherwise checked to see if it would work. Then again, it was hard to ignore 500,000 fans. Well, not that hard, actually. After a lot of back-and-forth, with Evan going so far as to say, "Just get it out—I don't even need to be paid—just get it out," Warner came back and said it would release the song on December 29. Why December 29? More "tried-and-true" internal processes had to be followed, coupled with the fact that the company's standard practice of releasing new music on Tuesdays pointed toward Tuesday, December 29.

Hello? Did anyone at Warner notice this was a Christmas song? Even though Warner executives had the capability of getting the song out by the second week of December, they finally released it on December 22. Results? It sold more downloads than all of his previously released music combined, music that *had* undergone the "tried-and-true" process of testing, refining, market research, and beyond. In fact, "Merry Swiftmas" became his first song to crack the *Billboard* top-selling list for "hot country."

According to Evan, had he gone through the normal "process," the label wouldn't have been able to cobble together a budget, let alone an actual release, before the season was long over. Why did he tell Warner he didn't need to be paid? Because he was more interested in having fans gain access to his music, fans who then might want to go to one of his shows, buy a T-shirt, and download even more music from iTunes.

Hard to fathom why Warner wouldn't want to follow the lead of someone who so clearly understands his market and who is clearly so much closer to the customer than any analyst sitting in an office somewhere in L.A. However, the story continues. Three months later, Evan sent copies of a new song he had just cut to 10 of the top radio stations in the country. Evan thinks this will be the lead song on his new album. Warner isn't so sure and wants to debate, study, and otherwise apply its standard process to this song as well.

Evan merrily sidestepped the process again, and the song got immediate play in the most popular time slots. Why? Because people everywhere knew him from his Christmas song. The radio stations soon were fielding a plethora of excited calls from fans asking where they could buy it. Bitter news: they can't buy the song because the process hasn't caught up yet.

Unless, of course, Evan has just invented a new process.

LET THEM INVENT THE WORKAROUND

My good friend Michael Winston has spent his career helping large organizations manage significant change in aerospace, technology, and financial services. Michael is both a psychologist and an M.B.A., so I always highly respect his insights. When I asked him to summarize the lessons, he did not hesitate for a second: "People do not like changes made *to* them but don't mind changes made *by* them. Just be sure to give them criteria with meaning and oversight." How's that for simple, direct, and to the point?

You may remember my friend Irwin Carasso from Chapter 4, the title of which says it all: how you frame the problem is the problem. Following is a great example of how someone else helped him see a puzzle and its solution, one that involved changing a process so that his workers would be better off. The change also produced an unexpected and very positive customer benefit.

In the early days of Tree of Life, the natural foods distribution company, Irwin had difficulty retaining people in certain positions. In particular, his order packers would turn over rather quickly. I had been working with Irwin and his employees on engagement and motivation issues, but I completely missed this wonderfully insightful workaround idea.

Order packers dragged tape machines, packing paper, and boxes from pallet to pallet around the warehouse, making certain that product count was accurate and then preparing the order for shipment and finally creating the bill of lading. No one seemed to care for the job. High turnover led to order inaccuracy and poorly packaged goods that sometimes arrived damaged.

A computer programmer and friend of Irwin's watched the order packers one day and offered an observation about why people would leave so quickly. He told Irwin that the job lacked dignity—dragging equipment around the shop floor seemed more like itinerant work and failed to give the workers a sense of belonging anywhere. The programmer suggested that Irwin give them their own work area and have the orders brought to them for packing.

Taking a cue from the engagement work we were doing, along with the suggestion from his programmer friend, Irwin sat down with the order packers over lunch one day and asked them what they thought about the idea. The order packers came up with even more ideas from the control side of the equation that both streamlined the job and made it more enjoyable to them.

Here's what transpired, in Irwin's own words:

> We followed the combination of advice from my computer friend and that of the packers, creating a separate packing station. My packers stayed for years (they were still there when I sold the company 10 years later). They trained and apprenticed their new employees to make sure all orders were packed and counted properly. The packing team took considerable pride in their work and often held meetings on their own to keep improving the process.
>
> One day, I got a call from a large customer in New Orleans, the Whole Food Company. The owner was Peter Roy, who later went on to become president of the Whole Foods chain. He called to tell me about the incredible quality of our orders, including the accuracy of each order and, in particular, the packaging. He told me that in the whole last year, he had not received one damaged product.

What a lovely and powerful story. Faced with a big turnover problem along with order inaccuracy and damaged goods in shipping, Irwin was able to solve several problems by the act of engaging the employees in the solution. In my consulting career, I cannot tell you how many times incredibly creative solutions have come from people on the front lines. It's unfortunate that more often than not, management tends to view the front line as cogs in the machine more interested in the paycheck than performance improvement.

Try engaging those on the line when performance issues arise and you may well find any number of workarounds. This advice may turn out to be particularly helpful when the process seems to be the problem. You may be surprised to discover just how many process improvements these folks can bring to bear—you just have to ask!

RELOCATE THE PROCESS

The following case has to do with a time-consuming and cumbersome decision process. The quality of decision wasn't the issue, nor was it the people making the decision (both of which had been under attack until a new program manager showed up).

In Chapter 9, we talked about the kind of negative decision making that many people employ, taking aim more often at what's wrong with an option than at how to move forward. In this case, the team was forward focused.

As it turned out, the real issue had to do with *where* decisions were being made, which greatly influenced how they were being made and how long it took to arrive at a solution! This example is a follow-on to one featured in Chapter 10. I'll set the scene again for you in the first three paragraphs before proceeding.

In the mid-1990s the U.S. Air Force commissioned a new, powerful missile-defense weapon that would require the development of a complex new technology. The prime contractor, Airco, had extensive experience building aircraft, while Satco had equal experience building space vehicles and advanced technologies. Their combined expertise looked like a perfect match for the new weapon system, which was to be deployed from aircraft in flight.

The multibillion-dollar program initially targeted testing in the early 2000s and full deployment by 2009. As is often the case in the aerospace world, the program ran into numerous schedule delays, some related to the complex technologies involved and some having more to do with relationships between the two contractors and the customer.

The initial test finally took place in 2007, several years late, but at least it worked. The customer agreed to go forward but with a much sharper focus on timing and budget for the second test. Among the most troubling issues that contributed to the multiple delays the first time around were inadequacies in information sharing, decision making, and communication. That would be par for the course. Just about every organization I have ever worked with endures some version of these three problem areas within its leadership and management ranks.

One part of the inner workings of the program that had held back performance the first time had to do with how the team resolved problems as they arose. In the trade, they call these problems "nonconformance issues." Typically, nonconformance issues required involvement and sign-off from 15 or so different specialists from the customer, Airco, and Satco. The groups were located in different cities miles apart from one another.

In itself, passing the information along to multiple sites would have been challenge enough. When you add to that three sub-teams, each needing to coordinate with others, the scheduling challenges for getting together created huge delays. The upshot was that each issue required an average of 76.5 days to resolve. When delays are measured in minimum increments of one million bucks per day, you can imagine that soon, you could be talking about serious money. Oh, and did I mention there were more than 2,000 nonconformance issues!

The quality of decisions and resolutions, as previously stipulated, was seldom the rub. It just took forever to resolve anything because of the geographic and scheduling nightmares. As the team on the ground brainstormed options to accelerate the schedule, it hit on a brilliant if not inexpensive answer: hire the 15 specialists specifically for the program and locate them literally outside the door of the aircraft, so that when an engineer discovered a problem, all he or she had to do was walk down the stairs and over to the conference room where the team was housed.

This idea virtually eliminated any challenges associated with scheduling across three organizations or handing off data back and forth across locales. Average time for resolution shrank from 76.5 days to 4.5 days. Hmm. Let's see, 2,000 issues × 76.5 days versus 2,000 issues × 4.5 days. The math sort of speaks for itself. Of course, it took some selling to get approval for another $4 million to $5 million in budget and head count. However, given just a little bit of math, the program manager was able to convince the brass that even if he cut the time only by half, the money would be more than well spent.

Well spent, indeed!

THEY JUST DON'T UNDERSTAND THAT THEY DON'T UNDERSTAND

Have you ever been in a situation in which you had discrete knowledge on how something worked but were obliged to abide by processes or decisions from someone lacking the same knowledge? The following reflects just that kind of disconnect.

Deborah works as a senior buyer of complex electronic goods used in certain defense systems. Much of her career has been with electronics firms. Her current employer, however, has a long history of manufacturing mechanical goods and therefore has employed buyers who negotiate contracts for mechanical goods. That also means it has processes geared toward mechanical purchasing requirements.

The buying processes for mechanical goods are very different from the buying processes for electronics, especially when your final product is destined to spin around in space. Deborah was hired because of her deep expertise in buying electronics that meet what in the trade is referred to as "mil-spec," short for "military specifications." Suffice it to say that mil-spec is precise, very precise. Especially for equipment that will eventually make its way into orbit.

Deborah's current challenge has to do with educating her purchasing organization on the ins and outs of buying electronics to mil-spec. Since no one else in the company has electronics mil-spec history, Deborah gets involved in purchasing everything from million-dollar contracts to five-dollar parts. The larger purchasing organization, which monitors how she spends her time, is currently agitated about how many hours she spends on buying small parts. As a level-three buyer, she is expected to focus on larger contracts, leaving the small potatoes to junior buyers.

Unfortunately, the company does not have junior buyers who understand what it takes to comply with mil-spec purchases. Does the phrase *catch-22* come to mind?

The good news is that the managers of the process organization (Six Sigma) understand that they need to develop processes that work for mil-spec electronics. However, since Deborah is the only person who understands what is required, the Six Sigma group needs her time and expertise to build the processes. It follows that when she is spending time on developing processes, she is not spending time on million-dollar contracts.

What do you do when you have multiple catch-22s? What Deborah will need to do in order to smooth out the dilemma is to first understand the various silos and what their residents' marching orders are. Then she will need to organize a summit, similar to that mentioned in Chapter 7 on silos.

COMMON WORKAROUND THEMES

The common threads that connect the musician, the packer, the aerospace team, and the mil-spec buyer all have to do with bringing solutions closer to the people who experience the problem and the opportunity firsthand. Too often it happens that processes and procedures start with information that emanates from people in direct contact with the challenge and then migrate over to specialists who have little or no contact whatsoever with the actual circumstances being addressed.

Much has been written on why process-improvement efforts come up short, with the most common theme being "resistance" to change by the people involved. My mentor used to tell me that resistance was typically a lack of understanding and that if you encountered resistance, the workaround was to develop understanding. Once people understand, they can usually go along.

Michael Winston's observation that "people do not like changes made *to* them but don't mind changes made *by* them" holds considerable weight here.

In the examples cited, the crux had less to do with what needed to be changed and more to do with who was in the best position to know. Irwin's packers were originally hired to do a job and then told how to perform the task. The instructions and processes all made sense from a management point of view, but not to the actual person who had to perform the task.

In the Airco and Satco example, executives far removed from the manufacturing facility reasoned that scientists and experts located at their respective HQs would be best suited to figure out resolutions. Of course, these executives were looking at the accuracy of resolutions, not the timing of resolutions. Asking the engineers on the ground what they needed was the impetus for a practical workaround that preserved the effectiveness of the resolutions but appreciably accelerated the timeliness factor.

In Deborah's case, the purchasing department does not fully understand the complexities of mil-spec and therefore needs expertise to guide its decisions. However, the group that understands the need for guidance is removed from the group monitoring how time is spent. When Deboarh devotes effort to helping develop the processes that will benefit everyone over time, she also gets dinged by the very group that hired her for her expertise.

When you're confounded by roadblocks, delays, low morale, or a host of other performance imbroglios, it may be best to stop and ask those on the front lines what the problem looks like from their vantage point. I realize that this qualifies as a pretty low-tech workaround, but it may just be the low-hanging fruit you're looking for. Too often in my experience, management spends considerable time and resources in conference rooms looking for complex, high-tech solutions when simple and effective solutions are staring them in the face. These solutions can often be had by simply engaging those who perform the work, where they perform the work.

FORM YOUR OWN SKUNK WORKS

If you are being waylaid by someone or something in your attempt to get something meaningful done, you may need to form your own version of a Skunk Works.

What's a Skunk Works, you ask? According to bnet.com, the term refers to "a fast-moving group, working at the edge of the organization structure, which aims to accelerate the innovation process without the restrictions of organizational policies and procedures. Skunk Works can operate unknown to an organization or with its tacit acceptance. With the organization's acceptance, Skunk Works can be an extreme form of intrapreneurialism." The term was popularized by Tom Peters and Nancy Austin in *A Passion for Excellence* (1985)."

Fast-moving—that's the point, isn't it? You want to accelerate the process, to get something done that matters, to accomplish something of consequence. There are dozens of examples of Skunk Works that work, beginning with how the original concept was first applied at Lockheed Aircraft Corporation and continuing on to even more unconventional approaches to getting things done.

The Lockheed-Martin website provides this explanation:

The Skunk Works® was formed in June of 1943 in Burbank, Calif. The Air Tactical Service Command (ATSC) of the Army Air Force met with Lockheed to express its need for a jet fighter. A rapidly growing German jet threat gave Lockheed an opportunity to develop an airframe around the most powerful jet engine that the allied forces had access to, the British Goblin. Lockheed was chosen to develop the jet because of its past interest in jet development and its previous contracts with the Air Force. One month after the ATSC and Lockheed meeting, a young engineer by the name of Clarence L. "Kelly" Johnson and other associate engineers hand delivered the initial XP-80 proposal to the ATSC. Two days later the go-ahead was given to Lockheed to start development and the Skunk Works was born, with Kelly Johnson at the helm.

The formal contract for the XP-80 did not arrive at Lockheed until October 16, 1943, some four months after work had already begun. This would prove to be a common practice within the Skunk Works. Many times a customer would come to the Skunk Works with a request and on a handshake the project would begin, no contracts in place, no official submittal process. Kelly Johnson and his Skunk Works team designed and built the XP-80 in only 143 days, seven less than was required.

What allowed Kelly to operate the Skunk Works so effectively and efficiently was his unconventional organizational approach. He broke the rules, challenging the current bureaucratic system that stifled innovation and hindered progress. His philosophy is spelled out in his "14 practices and rules" that he and his team followed. Many of these "rules" are still considered valid today.*

Although this approach was originally agreed to by Lockheed management, other organizations have discovered that versions of Skunk Works have emerged without management knowledge, much less agreement. What's fascinating about the Skunk Works approach is how many incredible innovations have arisen from small groups of dedicated employees who would not succumb to organizational paralysis or bureaucratic encumbrance.

Compaq Computer created a highly profitable server line by sidestepping corporate approval processes. Several years ago, a team of self-described "rogue" engineers decided that an ultrathin, high-speed server could be developed, even though the initial pro-

---

*Reproduced with permission from Lockheed Martin.

posal and funding request had been denied. Without funding, and working on their own time, the team of "rogue volunteers" found a way to use existing Compaq technologies from multiple programs to come up with a low cost, high performance machine.

The team worked off-hours and often resorted to "dumpsterdiving" for spare parts that they could use in building their prototype. Unburdened by the normal layers of project teams and management oversight, they were able to come up with a sound product in a relatively short time. The product they eventually presented, the AlphaServer DS10L, turned out to be a top seller.

There are countless other examples of companies that were saved from themselves by industrious, resourceful, committed employees who saw something that mattered and worked around the system to produce something of substance.

The Compaq example yielded a multimillion-dollar business with global reach. I'm told that SmithKline French wound up with the blockbuster Tagamet by essentially the same process—a team of research scientists ignored the rejection they received from the internal committee and went about producing the ulcer drug in a clandestine lab.

As you go about finding your own workarounds, you may need to enlist the support of others, or you may need to go it alone. You may be met with agreement, approval, or even collaboration when you propose a different way of getting things moving. It's also undeniable that you may encounter resistance, roadblocks, or even outright sabotage.

WORKAROUND QUESTIONS

When you're incapacitated by processes that plainly don't work, or when the person in charge lacks the necessary experience to understand the straits in which you've been placed, you may need to work on understanding the issue from the opposing perspective before you can light on a workaround strategy. Here are some questions to feed your thoughts:

1. What challenges do you face in getting your job done?

2. How is the organization making things more difficult than necessary?

3. What could you improve if you had support, permission, or cooperation?

4. What processes or procedures exist that don't seem to make sense?

5. How would you suggest the organization streamline its processes or procedures?

6. What information do you need that you don't have?

7. What information do you think others may need that they don't have?

8. What other groups, departments, or individuals should you be talking to?

9. How can you help remove roadblocks (for yourself or for others)?

16

Overcoming Criticism, Complaints, and Resistance

People can surely present challenges to one another through their mental and emotional attitudes. Perhaps you have noticed. Some of the more difficult attitudes to address are those that show up in the form of nonstop criticism, complaints, and plain old resistance. Nothing ever seems to be right, good enough, or well thought-out—these folks can find fault with anything. Often, these people would rather bellyache and moan than roll up their sleeves and do anything about the object of their discontent.

So, tell me, then, have you had your minimum daily requirement of criticism today? If so, have you also offered your share to people with whom you work or live? Do you know anyone whose core competency appears to be the ability to criticize or find fault with just about anything, any time? This criticism competency is an imbedded attribute of negative people and complainers everywhere. One of the biggest challenges to overcoming this criticism competency can be traced back to spelling tests. Seriously.

Say there were 50 words on the test, and you spelled 44 of them correctly. Now, is 44 out of 50 pretty good? Depends on your point of view, doesn't it? As a percentage, 44 out of 50 is 88 percent. As a grade, that's at least a B, maybe even B+ or A−. And what did the test paper say on top when you got it back? An unfortunately popular way for teachers to relay such a test score is with a "−6" in red ink. How encouraging is −6? How do you build on −6? Somehow −5 doesn't seem like improvement, whereas +45 feels a lot better. They are both the same data point, yet one is a deficit way of thinking and the other is more positive—kind of like the old half-empty, half-full argument.

And how many years did you go to school? How much −6 have you had in your life, in one form or another? Do you know anyone who hasn't had enough criticism already? In a perverse way of thinking, managers, coaches, teachers, parents, and just about all of us learned something about "helping" others from our spelling test experiences. Help comes in the form of "constructive criticism."

Really, though, who needs more criticism? Here's a general piece of advice that applies to just about every situation in which people interact: beware of the natural tendency to point out faults, the −6 stuff, whether it is you pointing out the missing pieces or someone pointing out your shortcomings. If you are the one noticing the deficit, you should strive to turn it into +44 feedback. If someone is pointing out your deficits, you can ask the person to turn the deficit into +44 feedback as well. The +44 approach is the same regardless of which side of the feedback equation you occupy, and it requires putting your finger on only two elements:

- What parts of this are working well? (+44)

- What would make this work even better? (How can you build on +44?)

Deficit thinking has helped us become a society in which getting better suggests that one must be inefficient or broken in the first place. I'm pretty sure you're not broken, so let's turn the concept into one of good and getting better. If you can treat other people from the mind-set of good and getting better, then you may find that all manner of negative interactions begin to dissolve.

CRITICISM CONUNDRUM

Some years ago, I was speaking to an audience of several hundred schoolteachers, and I shared this perspective about spelling tests. As I was coming to a close, I noticed two people near the front who looked to be increasingly in distress, and they were now engaged in a hushed discussion. I stopped the speech and inquired if they were OK. One of them said, "Well, yes and no." I asked what she meant, and that's when I got a big surprise.

"We team-teach and just had our midterm exam. One of our students had a perfect paper."

"OK," I said, confused. "So, what's the problem with a perfect paper?"

"Well, we gave the student the paper back and wrote -0 in red on the top!"

Everyone cracked up at first, and then the impact began to sink in. What kind of message does -0 send to the kids in the class? That if you happen to achieve perfection, we're still going to let you know that we're watching and you better not slip up? From there in the presentation, it was even easier for me to establish the main point: what are we teaching our children to become? If we grow up with "enough" criticism, do we learn to focus on improvement, or do we learn to focus on deficits? "Good and getting better" is a much better message than "Not good enough."

Managers would be wise to consider this the next time they have a performance review to administer. Why not start with asking what the employee did particularly well, followed by where the employee thinks he or she could do even better next time around? The manager can then follow up with personal observations.

If you have endured many performance reviews, you know for yourself how often the accent is on the negative. Most reviews that are done these days tend to have a few gratuitous positives, followed by a litany of −6 "areas for improvement." As with teaching kids in school, we do need to be able to speak the truth: if someone needs to improve, let's help the person get there. In that pursuit, burying people in more −6 criticisms won't do nearly as much for them as helping them build on what they are already doing well.

THE HIDDEN POWER OF COMPLAINTS

It's not just management that is capable of overemphasizing the negative; employees at virtually any level frequently engage in this behavior by complaining. Of course, complaints can be valid, but how about the person who seems to complain regularly? An atmosphere of complaining can poison the environment with an abundance of negativity, as well as meld into the culture and become its own form of roadblock. If you add a culture of complaint to a culture of consensus or buy-in, you can stop just about anything from moving forward.

From the perspective of upper management, complaints may run the gamut from enlightening to frustrating to downright hilarious. Do you know anyone who seems to belong to the "Ain't It Awful" club? You know the club: it typically meets during lunch, over coffee, or at the local pub after hours; membership requires the ability to complain and excel at "one-downmanship."

Members are very good at pointing out the faults of others and specialize in identifying the flaws of management and those in charge. Once one member gives voice to a problem, someone else is spurred to chime in with something even worse. "You think that's bad, wait until you get a load of this." The spiral continues until everyone is convinced that nothing will ever get any better.

Rarely is senior management interested in hearing all of these complaints and criticisms. Why? Because we tend to look kind of silly when in complaint mode. Just about anyone can see past the complaints to aspects of our own work that could be improved if only we would take the initiative to make the improvement.

Who wants to listen to the complaints of someone who won't take care of his or her own area of response-ability? However, the ground may shift when you fix what you can.

As we have established, if you can identify a problem and fix what you can on your own (control), you then may be able to influence others to join in by improving what they can. If you catch yourself complaining, you are probably noticing something that could be improved and just haven't got around to doing what can be done. As we have also established, the object of the first workaround you need may well be your own attitude and actions. Having gone as far as you can down that road, what can you do when confronted with the chronic complainer, especially when you need the complainer to get busy and do something?

How to Turn Complaints into Action

Complaints can reveal all kinds of hidden information if you can just get past the whining nature of most complainers. First of all, in order for someone to complain, what must be true? Probably a dozen things, but I'm looking at a couple in particular. The first is that the complainer has probably observed something that could be improved. Perhaps even less obvious is that the person cares enough to complain! At least the person is engaged enough to notice and to say something. That may seem trivial, but think about it for a moment.

For the most part, no one complains about things that can't be changed. My favorite example is gravity. Everyone "suffers" from gravity in one way or another. Ever trip and fall? You couldn't fall without gravity, now, could you? Do you ever hear anyone complaining about gravity? Are you either overweight or underweight? Couldn't be either without gravity. Ever notice that

either just ignore gravity or play with it. If you're wondering what
I mean by "play with it," I will refer you to the Olympics, wherein
people the world over get together and test their ability against
gravity. Who can jump the farthest, leap the highest, spin the
most, balance better than anyone else, throw something farther,
and so forth.

If you can accept my premise that we seldom complain about
something that can't be changed, then take the next mental leap
and consider that a complaint is simply a sign that the person
complaining would like to see something done differently and just
hasn't taken the steps necessary to engage with the improvement.

In an odd way, the complainer may be hoping that complaining will be sufficient, rather than actively working toward a solution—which is what this book is all about.

Three Types of Complainers, One Workaround

While many complainers are unique in their own ways, most tend
to come in one of three varieties: the technical complainer (TC),
the professional complainer (PC), and the generalist complainer
(GC). TCs have the ability to notice essentially anything and
everything that is out of spec. If there's a fault, they can find it.
TCs are good to have around if finding faults matters. For example, TCs can be quite helpful in your quality-inspection process.
They may not be terribly good at fixing the faults, but at least they
can zero in on them.

A close relative of the TC is the PC—the professional complainer. PCs tend to also notice faults, but at a level higher than
mere technical faults. The PC will notice systemic issues, process
issues, or larger organizational issues. PCs can also be useful, but
they can be irritating at the same time. It seems that the PCs of

the world attribute more value to their complaints than do those who have to hear them. Both the PC and TC offer valid criticisms, and the insightful manager or coworker can look past the whining nature of the complaint or the seemingly constant barrage of criticism and expose that validity.

The third category of complainer presents a different challenge. The GC, or generalist complainer, has no territorial limit; these ladies and gentlemen have built a core competency around complaint and criticism and can poke holes in darn near anything. They also tend to be pretty sharp, although their true brilliance may be masked by the near constant whining and their unparalleled skill in one-downmanship.

Negatives aside, even the GCs are trying to tell you something that could be useful. In order to complain, they usually must first perceive something that could be improved, most likely something that could be of some importance; they just aren't engaged or secure enough to take action themselves. In fact, if you ask most complainers, regardless of type, they will tell you that by complaining, they think they are doing something. For them, complaining equates to action.

Next time you hear a complaint coming from someone, especially if it's you, ask one or more of these questions:

- What would you prefer instead?

- Why would it matter?

- Who would benefit if this improved?

- What would it look like if this were different?

- What would it take to make this better?

Any of these or dozens of variants will work wonders. Keep in mind that the complaint is in essence a signal that the complainer can see something that could be improved. Sometimes complainers are actually right and just don't know how to get the message across or, worse, don't think anyone else cares. If they are right, and you ask them one of these questions, you can change the conversation from the typical bitch session to something productive. If you go down this inquiry route, you can follow up with questions that represent the control and influence circles:

- What could you do to help improve the situation all on your own?

- What could you do to help improve the situation with support, collaboration, or approval from someone else? Who?

- What do you need in order to help improve this situation?

- How can I help?

The key is to recognize that hidden inside the complaint, there may well be a nugget of value. You don't need to waste time with those who just complain as an excuse to avoid taking action, but then you may want to know what's in the way, if, indeed, something is in the way. By asking a few of these kinds of questions, you can interrupt the pattern of complaining that saps productivity—your productivity, their productivity, and perhaps that of the whole organization. If you are sincere in the questions you ask, you may just discover something important and wind up encouraging employees to move from complaint to positive action. Embracing complaints may be a way to reduce the amount of them, uncover meaningful improvement opportunities, and turn marginal employees into productive ones.

Workaround Ideas: Dealing with Complainers

Here are a couple of ways to break through resistance when people are complaining:

- **Redirect their complaints into roles or tasks that take advantage of the complaint.** Both the TC and PC can present interesting mini-workaround opportunities. Assuming that their faultfinding tends to be reasonably accurate, one way to turn the incessant criticism into something of value is to retrain the TC or PC for a role within your quality-inspection process. Hey, if they are good at finding faults, you may as well have them finding faults that matter!

- **Engage them in the job of fixing the problem.** Give them permission, authority, and sufficient air cover to encourage their active participation in stamping out the menace. Sometimes complainers would truly like to get involved, but they fear that they will be struck down or become the target of criticism themselves if their ideas don't work perfectly the first time. Be sure to remove the fear of punishment if their ideas don't work.

HOW TO OVERCOME RESISTANCE

A colleague and I were flying out of Chicago, and the snow was blowing hard. Flights were canceled all over the country, including our flight. We were doing our best to get to the client site for a meeting the next morning, but things were not looking hopeful. We had boarded our flight only to learn shortly thereafter that it was canceled. We made a beeline to the customer service counter and were second in line. The "gentleman" in front of us moved up to the counter and started laying into the agent. He was angry beyond angry.

As the agent was checking for flight options, the passenger grew increasingly impatient and ever more belligerent. After only a minute or two, he launched into the old "Do-you-know-who-I-am-and-how-much-I-fly" line. Of course the agent had some clue, having full access to the guy's record.

As the decibel level rose and the derogatory words for the agent increased, the agent looked up at him and said, "Sir, there are only two people I can think of right now who care about your situation, and one of them is fast losing interest."

Now, there's an all-time line if ever there was one. It's baffling how some people can think that bullying the other person is the way to get what they want. This passenger walked away with a coach ticket for a flight the next morning. When we got to the counter, Mark looked at the agent and said with all sincerity, "You must have an impossibly difficult job. So many people must think they are the most important person in your world, and I just can't imagine how you handle that kind of abuse."

He then presented our tickets and told her we were in the same pickle as the guy before us. She looked at Mark, thanked him for his understanding, hammered at the keyboard for a few minutes, and then said, "As I told the other gentleman, I'm afraid we don't have anything left tonight in our inventory; however, if you don't mind first class, I can get you there on another airline."

What a neat example of thinking about what matters to the other person when you are trying to influence that person. In this case, all it took was sensitivity to the agent's position and treating her in a manner that communicated that sensitivity.

Regardless of the situation, the other person has something that's important to him or her. Whether you're working with a customer service agent during a weather snafu or dealing with a reluctant team member back at the office, remember that most people have a reason for their choices.

Even if the other guy seems irrational, that's probably not how that individual sees the situation. When pitted against people who are not cooperating, ask yourself why their choices might make sense to them. What might the underlying reason be? What might be important to this person in this situation? If you can conjure one or two possibly helpful explanations, you may change your tone a bit, and the other person may loosen up a bit and become more open to influence. You will be pretty safe in assuming that the other person is making choices that he or she perceives will work best in the long run. Seeking to understand what motivates the other guy will serve you well.

When Your Support Team Resists

How often have you been flummoxed by someone in another group or department whose support you need and who is apparently uninterested in helping? In fact, sometimes the other person, group, or department may seem to be deliberately working against you. Meanwhile, what looks like resistance to you may be something altogether different to the other party. Here's an example of how I learned that lesson many years ago.

In my first job out of college, I had an entry-level sales position at Pacific Telephone, in San Francisco. My job was to call on small and medium-size businesses to assess their telecommunications needs and sell them newer, more advanced systems. In my first few days of classroom orientation and training, I kept hearing stories about how difficult the people in Plant could be. The stories all carried the same basic message: "Watch out—they'll screw you every time." Some attributed this antagonism to Plant's being unionized, while people in Sales were considered to be management.

I figured, OK, that may be true, but why not find out what's really going on—from *their* point of view? I asked my boss if I could go on some installations with the Plant field teams so I could see firsthand what the work was like from their perspective. When I went over to the dispatch area to meet with my first crew, I was greeted with more than a little cynicism. "What's the college boy want with us working folks?" and, well, maybe a bit rougher, actually. I persisted, letting them know that I'd heard that Sales could make it difficult for them but didn't really know how, that I wanted to learn, and that I would be happy to take any instruction they had for me. Turning the issue around—Sales may be the problem, not Plant—worked pretty well.

Perhaps a bit reluctantly, but grinning inside, they let me tag along on some installations. That's when I saw a huge difference between what we learned in the classroom and what real life was like. The classroom showed us how to write an order and how to make a diagram indicating where phones and switchboards would go. What it didn't teach us was the difference between the theoretical and the possible.

The first installation I went on with the guys from Plant had a nicely drawn-up order and diagram, but these materials didn't take into consideration how all the wires were going to get to that location—old building, solid concrete walls, no way to pull cable. The next installation needed more lines than the building had available. More of the same showed up with virtually every order I saw.

After a couple of days, I formed a pact with the guys in Plant. Before writing anything that looked the least bit complicated, I would ask for a field visit to confirm what was possible. Field visits were akin to pulling teeth, and Plant had a history of dragging its feet getting out to the site. In my case, as soon as I had a sense of what might be good for the customer, I would call Plant, and usually within a couple of hours, someone would show up with me to take a look. My orders had a way of flying through Plant, often beating the published installation time lines. I made it a regular practice to go down to dispatch at least once a month and ask around—"Any problems with the orders I'm writing? Am I doing anything that makes your job more difficult?" The college kid trotted off with some essential support from those not-so-gruff Plant guys.

In almost any situation in which you encounter resistance, what you may actually be facing is people who care about their jobs and how your involvement might get in *their* way! When faced with apparent resistance, start by asking yourself what the situation looks like from the other guy's standpoint. Once you are privy to that perspective, you may discover unforeseen work-around opportunities, many of which will lead to improved collaboration and mutual support.

TREAT THEM LIKE THE INTELLIGENT PEOPLE THEY ARE!

My longtime friend Patrick Carroll owns a small insurance bro-kerage firm in Southern California that is doing quite well now, which wasn't the status a few years back. Patrick learned that his real success would come from his people, not from his business.

His employee benefits and personal insurance firm was "in shambles" seven years ago after his partnership collapsed. He knew he needed to do something fast and began looking at a new sales and marketing program. As he told me then, "No one really wants insurance; in fact, people *hate* insurance. It's confusing, it's expensive, and it forces them to look at outcomes no one wants to think about."

The more he thought about it, the more he realized that the issue had less to do with people's not wanting insurance and more to do with their not understanding it. It slowly became apparent that the only way to sell something that no one understands is to help people learn. Then it hit him: he was actually in the education business! If his firm was going to be successful, the members would have to become educators, not just salespeople.

Once Patrick reframed the problem, eschewing trying to sell when he needed to educate instead, he realized that the next problem that needed to be worked around was himself. He had been mostly hands-on as a manager, often micromanaging the smallest of tasks. Given that his office employs a grand total of three people, including himself, it's understandable that he would be hands-on. However, Patrick was aware that if the newly reframed business was going to succeed, he would need to let go of his sales mind-set and adopt an entirely new way of going about his business.

That's when he stumbled on the most important ingredient for his future success: his people. As he told me recently, "The real secret turned out to be my two employees. Once I had communicated the new educational company vision, all I had to do was get out of their way. I needed to trust them and get over my owner's mind-set that I had to micromanage everything."

Patrick's role turned from control to support; his job became one of learning what his two-person team needed and then providing that support. Frequently, that meant removing roadblocks, including those of his own making, and thereby letting them succeed.

Within just a couple of months, they had made a 180-degree turn, and their phones started ringing and haven't stopped. In the seven-year period from cratered partnership to this writing, his business is up 400 percent, his customer retention rate is well over

90 percent, and his employees love the impact they continue to have on the business.

The Power of Recognition

Marshall Goldsmith has authored many books on leadership. Two of my favorites, *What Got You Here Won't Get You There* and his newest, *Mojo*, contain some excellent pieces of advice that add context and enhancements to workarounds. One tip that he offered me for this book has to do with employee engagement, or employee involvement. Often, managers and supervisors think they have to poke, prod, or otherwise encourage people to get them to perform well. In the case of Irwin Carasso's packers from the preceding chapter, both employee performance and employee retention were predominantly linked to letting staff contribute to the job they were hired to do.

Job descriptions tell people what to do and usually how to do it. While that can be important, especially in highly technical or dangerous jobs, Marshall would tell us that we can often fare a lot better by turning job descriptions into results the employee is responsible for producing instead of simply delineating tasks. If you provide a description of results expected, you can also provide a basic template for job activity, processes, or procedures to help employees get started, but let them know that you can imagine them coming up with even more effective ways to get the job done. Encouraging them to take ownership of the outcome corresponds with the guidelines provided in Chapter 6 on accountability and response-ability.

Marshall told me that managers often fret about how to recognize employees for their contributions and typically default to bonuses, awards, certificates, or letters from someone higher up. While these are nice, they may not be enough to keep people motivated and engaged for long. Rather than trying to figure out how you can recognize someone, try asking the person instead.

Although Patrick did not have the benefit of Marshall's personal coaching, he nonetheless came up with an approach similar to what Marshall might have advocated, asking his employees questions along the lines of these:

1. What have you been doing particularly well?

2. What are you doing that I am unlikely to notice?

3. What could you do even better if you had more support?

4. What roadblocks do we place in your way?

5. What improvements could you imagine making to our processes?

6. What do customers seem to notice or care about?

7. How could we do an even better job of acknowledging you and your team?

Asking these kinds of questions may provide more recognition and have more impact than just about anything else you can do.

COMMON PEOPLE PROBLEMS AND WORKAROUNDS

Impediments of all shapes abound in day-to-day life. Here's one thing I've learned about ineffective process, misaligned priorities, broken technologies, and just about any other impediment you can name: the problem usually starts with people. This section takes you through a hit list of common people issues and workarounds to get past them.

1. People succumb to that's-just-the-way-we-do-things-around-here kind of thinking.

2. People can operate from that's-not-my-job as well as that's-not-your-job attitudes.

3. People can become downright stubborn when it comes to change.

4. People can be risk averse, seeking perfection over direction.

5. People get stuck in resistance, often because they lack understanding.

6. People sometimes just want you to fail so they can appear superior or right.

7. People can . . . well, people can do just about anything.

People Succumb to That's-Just-the-Way-We-Do-Things-Around-Here Kind of Thinking

In Chapter 2, we had you cleaning a refrigerator. One of the reasons you wound up cleaning that refrigerator is that you have a personal standard about what a refrigerator is supposed to do (keep food fresh) and how it's supposed to look (clean).

When you notice something falling short of your own standard, you are likely to do something about it. Can you help people develop new standards that include the kinds of efficiencies or improvements you would prefer?

If so, they will respond in admirable ways. Citing Michael Winston yet again: "People do not like changes made *to* them but don't mind changes made *by* them. Just be sure to give them criteria with meaning and oversight." This is also what Patrick Carroll discovered in helping his insurance brokerage turn around.

People Can Operate from That's-Not-My-Job as Well as That's-Not-Your-Job Attitudes

If people refuse to budge either because it's not their job or because they object to your involvement, you may want to refer to Chapter 7, where we discussed some of these situations. The principle to keep in mind is that people do things for *their* reasons, not *your* reasons. Keep asking yourself why their choices might make sense to them.

For all you know, the answer could relate to how comfortable they are with risks or how they are being measured and rewarded. Once you understand what is important to them, you may discover options that include how you can help them, not just how they can help you. Be sure to ask yourself our favorite question: What can you do to make a difference that requires no one's permission other than your own?

People Can Become Downright Stubborn When It Comes to Change

"People do not like changes made *to* them but don't mind changes made *by* them."

If you are going to create change of some stripe, you can give yourself a running start by involving those who will be impacted by that change in its design and development. The more engaged people are in creating the new order, the more they will own it and get on board with making it happen.

You may also need to keep in mind the start-stop-continue advice in Chapter 2. Sometimes that apparent resistance stems from a plate that is already overflowing—they simply lack the mental or physical space to see a way forward. If you can remove items from people's to-do lists, you may find increasing receptivity.

People Can Be Risk Averse, Seeking Perfection over Direction

Establishing a sense of safety in the shadow of involvement or risk taking can be a means of working around roadblocks of one kind or another. Remember that most of us encounter way more "–6" feedback than we would prefer and that criticism leads people to hang back rather than risk more negative commentary.

Incorporating the kind of weekly review that we talked about in Chapter 11 may also prove helpful. Regular reviews can promote the distinction between direction and perfection that we talked about in Chapter 2.

Keep building on progress made rather than roadblocks encountered.

People Get Stuck in Resistance, Often Because They Lack Understanding

People often resist something that they don't understand. What appears to be outright resistance may be a steady signal that the person doesn't know what to do or where to turn. This is pretty much the epiphany Patrick Carroll had about selling insurance: if you sell, they will resist—if you educate, they will learn.

What underlies most lack of understanding and accompanying resistance is a fear of being harmed in some way. It's like the first time you summoned the nerve to jump off the high dive: it can look too scary until you see your peers do it. Getting some instruction first can help, and if people can take a few baby steps, they may gain enough confidence to take the bigger ones.

People Sometimes Just Want You to Fail So They Can Appear Superior or Right

This one can be tough. Have you ever heard the phrase *dead right*? Well, that's just how far some people will go in order to appear right. They will "fight to the death." These are also the people who will tell you that "it's just business—nothing personal."

Cloaked beneath all these defense mechanisms you will usually find someone who is fearful of losing something—respect, self-image, sense of contribution, or maybe even his or her job. These are big deals all by themselves and are the subjects of aisles full of books. Clearly, these are not the focus of this book.

However, workarounds for this kind of difficulty can sometimes be found in switching the −6 norms to +44 kinds of feedback. If you can blend +44 with directionally correct, and if people don't mind changes made by themselves, you may be able to transform resistance into the assistance you need.

WORKAROUND QUESTIONS

Working around people-oriented issues can be a yeoman's job. One of my favorite disarming questions when people complain about other people is to ask, "So, how many late-night hours do you think they spend trying to figure out new ways to mess with you?" It's a rare creature, after all, that participates in premeditated difficulty—not unheard of, just rare.

A few perspicacious questions can aid you when criticism, complaints, and resistance threaten to wear you down:

1. When the eternal critic comes knocking, first thank the person for caring enough to say something, and then ask questions:

   - What part of this is already working well?

   - What would it look like if the improvement took place?

   - Is there particular advice or support your critic can offer?

2. If you need to point out an area of improvement to someone, engage the person first in the solution before jumping in with your suggestions. Employ the sequence of intention, control, and influence in the conversation:

   - Intention: How does the person see this area working?

   - Control: Is there anything the person can see that he or she could do independently?

   - Influence: Is there anything he or she could do with support from someone else?

3. If it's the whiner-complainer on your horizon, start by acknowledging that the person must care in order to voice this comment—a disarming way to change the tone from whining to caring. Then ask questions as in the preceding situation:

   - Intention: What could the person imagine being different? How important is it to the person that this improvement be made?

   - Control: What could the person do independently?

   - Influence: What could he or she do with support or cooperation?

4. When faced with apparent resistance, reframe the observation: what must the person be perceiving in order to behave

that way? In addition to the standard intention, control, and influence questions, consider these:

- What is in the person's way?

- How does that impact him or her?

- How can you contribute to the improvement?

17

Multitasking Our Way to Oblivion

Increasing numbers of people seem to be increasingly proud of their ability to multitask even as growing research indicates that most multitaskers are actually less efficient and less accurate than their comparatively plodding tortoise cousins, the serial taskers. Before we dig into this juicy subject, though, let's go over a little science.

THE SCIENCE OF MULTITASKING

If your computer is running right now, you may have an e-mail program checking for messages, a browser tab or two open, a Word document in progress, and a PowerPoint presentation waiting there to be fine-tuned. Sure, the computer is multitasking, but you aren't! It may take only a mouse click or two to toggle between windows, but you still have to make the shift in order to access the benefit of those multiple programs. Even if you have two or three screens running, each displaying a different program, you still have to focus on one and then the other in order to get something done.

Just as with computers, your brain has the ability to crash, only for different reasons. And multitasking brains are subject to some interesting crashes. Indeed, your brain can shift quickly between windows, just not as well as the computer can. Researchers such as Dr. René Marois, at Vanderbilt University; Dr. Grit Hein, of UC Berkeley; and Dr. Paul Dux, of the University of Queensland, have made some intriguing discoveries about how the brain functions when attempting to focus on multiple tasks at the same time. In fact, current research shows that the multitasking brain is prone to big-time memory losses. It takes only a few hundred milliseconds for the brain to shift, and a select few super-multitaskers can shift even faster. However, most people's brains seem to prefer about a full second or two between shifts of focus.

The Hurrier I Go, the Behinder I Get

Neurologists have discovered a region of the brain, called the posterior lateral prefrontal cortex (pLPFC), that seems to be the central actor in the phenomenon of multitasking. This region functions much like a router, sorting information and distributing it where it belongs. However, the brain just can't process all the information simultaneously. Rather, imaging scans show that the pLPFC sticks the data in a queue and processes them serially.

Now, here's where the really bad news starts to show up for the multitasker: as processing intervals shorten and approach the 300-millisecond range, the brain actually slows down! In fact, when the pLPFC is slammed with multiple pieces of data to process, it appears to queue two for processing and drop the rest. The stuff that slips by the pLPFC goes to a part of the brain responsible for habitual learning, not the more cognitive kind that real processing and understanding require. To make matters worse, if you are trying to hold a conversation while reading text of some kind, then you are creating a major logjam on the internal information highway.

Josh Clark, senior writer for HowStuffWorks.com, had this to say about multitasking, in an article published at the Huffington Post:

If the pLPFC is busy processing other information, then the page we scanned, the bit of music we listened to, the question we were just asked, essentially slips past to the striatum. When we attempt to recall the information, it's not where it's supposed to be. In effect, the information came in, but it wasn't learned. It's the reason we're insulted when a person we're speaking to checks his BlackBerry while we're talking. We've entered into competition for the person's attention and, for the time being, we've lost. . . . Researchers have consistently drawn the same conclusion: multitasking is counterproductive and exhausting. Slll-loooowwww dooooowwwwwn.

Same thing goes for the husband reading the newspaper while his wife is trying to talk to him. "Yes, dear" is not the same as having heard or acknowledged the input, and you're bound to be caught.

WHAT MAKES MULTITASKING SEEM SO NECESSARY?

I realize that multitasking has become a way of life for many among us, and that's altogether understandable. So many things out there require our attention. We have personal goals, professional goals, career goals, financial goals, health goals, family goals, and on and on. We can have dozens of projects that require our attention, and to-do lists can drag on for pages.

Many of us don't seem to have enough time for things that really matter, including family, relationships, or even our own health. The notion of trying to get several things done at once not only seems to make sense but also seems to be a necessity of life. For some, multitasking has emerged as the new key to productivity. Or, at least the new key to busy-ness, for indeed, the multitasker is always busy.

It's somewhere between curious and sad watching people on the beach in Hawaii busily thumbing away while the whales swim by, scarcely able to even notice the relaxation they came there to find. A close second is watching a couple on a date, one or both of whom can be seen repeatedly pulling out an iPhone or Black-

Berry in order to stay in touch with someone who isn't there, all the while losing touch with the one who is.

People multitask everywhere these days, including BlackBerrying away during meetings, texting while driving, and talking on the phone while answering e-mail. Seems as if everyone's doing it.

Is Time Management the Problem?

Back in the early 1980s when David Allen and I created the *Managing Accelerated Productivity* seminar, the predecessor to *Getting Things Done*, we were often asked to help organizations with time-management problems. While we gratefully accepted the opportunities, we also liked to point out that if time management were the goal, then we were all going to be in big trouble.

Here's why: What can you do to time? Can you mismanage it so badly that hours shrink and you end up with fewer minutes? Can you become a black belt and end up with more hours than anyone else? Of course not. What people generally mean when they say they have a time-management problem is that they have a self-management problem. Somehow that doesn't seem quite so palatable, though. What we're really trying to do is become both more efficient with our use of time and more effective in terms of what we get out of it.

Solutions have been found all over the map, including speed-reading, ignoring messages until the person calls back the third time (honest to God, I have heard this one touted as an effective solution), and holding meetings while standing up. You get the idea. All kinds of tips rain down, but nothing really gets to the core. Today multitasking seems to be the current cure for what ails your time. The rationale must go something like, if you can chew gum and walk at the same time, surely you can process e-mail and take a phone call at the same time.

I know we can all walk and chew gum at the same time, but multitasking is different. What I'm talking about is akin to having your neurosurgeon texting while operating. If you're good with that, no need to read further! There are all kinds of multitaskers out there. Some are commonplace, others more exotic and polished. Almost none of them are half as effective as they might think. David and I like to say that the primary issue is one of focus management. It's not time management, or information overload, or just plain having more to do than you can ever hope to accomplish. It's focus.

THE DISTRACTED TASKER AND THE POWER TASKER

Here's a scenario that may present a window on your world: You sit down at your desk or workstation fully intending to take care of that little task that has been niggling you for some time now. As you get into it, you suddenly remember that you owe Sally a call, so while still assessing what needs done on that task, you ring Sally. She answers and then asks you to hold for a second. You say OK, and as you get back to the task, you notice a sticky note hanging from the computer reminding you to do something urgent two days ago. You suck in a deep breath and begin composing an e-mail to handle that chore. As you get into the e-mail, you notice another e-mail just arriving from someone you have been trying to contact for the past few days, so you open that message.

Now you have the initial task, Sally still on hold, the e-mail you're writing, and another e-mail that just arrived, when you hear a voice on the phone saying, "Hello." Inside, you go, "OMG—Hello, who?" And the day is only 10 minutes old!

If you keep this up, soon what started with that one little task and a couple of minor distractions blossoms into a half dozen or more open items spread around you, and there they remain all day long as you bounce around between distractions, getting some things done, and back to the distractions. When the day finally draws to a close, that one little task is still there, still not finished, and yet you have probably seen it, touched it, and started to work on it a good 5 to 10 times. You just kept forgetting to complete it.

Have you been there? C'mon—it's OK—we all have at least once. It's just that nasty old posterior lateral prefrontal cortex again! After only a few minutes of multitasking, you can get lost and forget where it was you started. It's not that you didn't get anything done; it's just that you didn't finish what you started and probably sucked away more than enough time to have handled it if you had just been focused enough to stick with it for the extra two minutes it would have taken.

For some, the scenario just described hardly qualifies as multitasking. Instead, that's just something akin to morning stretching, limbering up for the real stuff to come later. It's not so much multitasking gone awry as it is just flitting from one thing to the next without the benefit of much focus. The distracted tasker, as exemplified here, "works" all day long, is often tired, and typically feels a bit frustrated. It's as if you went to that refrigerator in Chapter 2 a dozen times and kept noticing the dry, scummy brown stuff, and the surfaces still aren't clean—but you do have things spread out all over the place, so it at least looks as if you've been busy.

Then there's the power tasker. Power multitaskers can run two or three BlackBerries simultaneously, jump on a conference call, take another call while still on the conference call, read an e-mail, and bark orders to an assistant or two, all while you're sitting in front of them for your long-scheduled meeting. They're also good at calling meetings and making you wait, and then when you finally do get under way, they manage to take every call that comes in, all the while signaling to you that you should keep going. But they do make eye contact!

I'm not making that up. I have actually been in this situation. Several times. And the person thinks he or she is doing a great job! What tends to escape the person's notice is that none of the seven or so things being handled simultaneously is being handled well. Many times, what was supposedly addressed the first time around needs to be dealt with again because something was missed or not handled appropriately.

The power tasker can finish a day (usually well into the evening) feeling as though a lot was accomplished. Different from the distracted tasker, however, is the frustration level. The power tasker may not feel frustrated, just tired. The frustrated people are all those who had to put up with two BlackBerries, simultaneous meetings, and constant interruptions.

If the object of the game is effective performance, it's probably obvious that working while distracted isn't a good tactic any more than driving while texting is a good idea. Perhaps less obvious is the impact of the power multitasker on performance: this person may feel that things are getting done, but everyone else in the equation is slowed down enormously.

THE MULTITASKER AND THE HALF-TASKER

While most people call it multitasking and seem proud of their ability, I call it "half-tasking." I'm sure you have heard the term *half-assed* used to describe an ineffective swipe at getting something done. I prefer "half-tasked." Half their attention is on one goal, and half their attention is on another. If you have only half your attention on something, then there's an excellent chance that the result will be "half-assed."

There are multiple challenges associated with multitasking, ranging from having your attention split between two or more tasks and not handling either one efficiently, to the annoyance you can cause others either through lack of consideration or by just plain wasting their time. Ever notice how frazzled multitaskers can seem? Some can be edgy to the utmost, wavering between irritated by all that they have to do and irritating in how they go about getting it done.

Hang in there—hope is on the way.

Workaround: Stop Half-Tasking and Start Multi-Goaling

Of course you have multiple things to do. That's a good thing. In fact, if you didn't have multiple things to do, you might be nearing the end of an active life. Even if you've lost your job, and I know what that one's like, you still have multiple things to do. More accurately stated, you have multiple goals you are seeking to accomplish, each of which requires multiple tasks in order to complete.

Can you hold multiple goals at the same time? Of course you can.

Can you work on multiple goals at the same time? Of course you can.

Can you work on multiple tasks at the same time? Well, that's another story.

Over the years, I have coached many executives who consider themselves to be power multitaskers, apparently able to keep a whole lot of balls in the air at the same time. Now, if keeping the balls in the air were the goal, that would be great. However, those balls represent actions that need to be completed on the way to accomplishing the real goal. Keeping actions in the air, or juggling multiple actions at the same time, is not the same as completing those actions.

When I can get people to focus on one task at a time, they typically become overtly excited about how much they can actually get done. To-do lists shrink, and, more important, goals and projects get completed. On time, even! People who are multi-goaling understand that they have any number of goals that are important to them. Maintaining health, launching a new product, finding a new job, finishing your taxes, and setting up a service project with your kid's school are all examples of goals that can be held simultaneously; however, each of them requires distinct actions, most of which are incompatible with one another.

Of course, every goal requires a number of tasks or actions to be completed. The challenge is how to keep your eye on the prize (accomplishing the goals that are most meaningful) while handling the dozens, if not hundreds, of actions that are on your plate.

Here's a seven-step workaround formula that may help you work around your own well-intentioned but often frustrating tendency to multitask:

1. **Focus on purpose or value: clarify what it is you are trying to accomplish and why.** Clarify which areas of life are most

important to you (health, wealth, personal growth, spiritual growth, relationships, family, career, service, etc.). What is it that you want, and what are you hoping to experience as a result? That's an important distinction right there: just look at what you are focused on and why it's important to you, and you may find that some goals or tasks promptly go away because they aren't really all that important. Most of us know the air-out-of-the-balloon experience that comes from wanting something really badly, working like crazy to finally get it, and then wondering why we ever wanted it. Do yourself a favor and take some time with this step; clarify not just what you want but also why you want it. Once you know the why, you may either abandon some of these "goals" or discover important parts of the process to pay attention to while getting there.

2. **Focus on your goals: what will it look like when you get there?** Identify the areas of life that are most important to you, and set a clear goal or two for each area you name. Don't underestimate these first two focus steps. There's an old country cliché that matters here: If you don't know where you are going, any road will do.

3. **Focus on next actions: make a list of actions you can take that will move you toward each of your goals.** Don't get obsessive about having to figure out *all* the steps for each goal. At a minimum, all you really need is to know where you are now and the very next step required to move toward that goal.

4. **Create separate lists for each key area.** Now that you know what's important to you, keep one list of your important goals, another list of projects you will have to complete in order to move you toward each goal, and a third list of action steps from which you can choose at any one time.

5. **Focus on small things: it's a cinch by the inch—make a little progress each day.** As you move through the day, pick off

action steps that you can accomplish now, with the resources you have available at the time, and then move to the next. One of my big lessons has been to break my list of tasks into lists of like actions. I have a phone list, for example. The phone list can have phone calls about several different goals or projects, but everything on the list is a phone call. The governing factor is that you actually need access to a phone to do anything on the phone list. Other lists might include one that requires Internet access, one for errands, one for things that you need to do at home, and one for things to do when you're in your St. Louis office. Long combined lists don't help much; there's no need to be looking at your list of actions to do at home when you're at work, unless you have to do something during the workday that pertains to something personal, such as making a doctor's appointment for your child.

6. **Have a "Mind like Mush" List.** One of my absolute favorite lists is "Mind like Mush." I use this list for various tasks that don't require much mental acuity and aren't critical in their timing. I turn to this list when my brain is drained. I get to knock off a few items with little risk of screwing them up because I'm not sharp—and an amazing thing happens most of the time: by knocking off a few simple items, I seem to catch a second wind and can then focus on more important tasks. This one will make more sense once you try it, especially if you remember the discussion in Chapter 2 about cleaning the refrigerator.

7. **Review and update your lists regularly.** Once a week, review your goals list to be certain you are making progress. Similarly, review your projects list to ensure you have a grip on those as well. As I've mentioned before, implementing a weekly review (Chapter 11) is an invaluable workaround.

Here are other tips that can help you manage your focus and become a master uni-tasker and supreme multi-goaler:

1. Remember your e-mail workarounds.

   a. Turn off your e-mail "you have mail" indicator sounds so you can stay focused.

   b. Schedule specific times each day to read and respond to e-mail, and put that information in your e-mail signature line.

   c. Let people know your standard for responding to e-mail, and put that in your signature line.

2. Schedule time for working on specific projects, letting your phone go to voice mail and saving e-mail for your scheduled processing time. Caution: if you told people they could reach you by cell phone if it's urgent, do answer the cell phone, but use your caller ID to screen those calls.

3. If you are constantly interrupted, consider finding a conference room, an empty cube, or even a space in the cafeteria where you can bang out work without interruptions.

4. Handle one item at a time, with nothing else in front of you—not your computer screen, no stacks of paper, nothing except the item you are handling and any reference material you need to support the task.

5. Conduct your weekly review. Besides keeping you current and ensuring that nothing slips through the cracks, it will reassure you that progress is being made and make it increasingly more acceptable to follow this kind of approach.

6. Buy a copy of Tony Schwartz's book *The Way We're Working Isn't Working.* Tony will give you further tips on managing your ability to transform the way you work. Great insights here!

7. Buy a copy of David Allen's bestselling book *Getting Things Done.* This book will help you set up a clean and elegant system for keeping track of your goals, projects, and next actions.

If you would like to become an effective high-performer, focus will become an increasingly important key to your success. If you have become a multitasker, a half-tasker, or a distracted tasker, then you may need to develop a few workarounds for your own habits!

WORKAROUND QUESTIONS

Changing work habits, especially ingrained habits such as multi-tasking, mandates real focus and commitment. If you choose to work on working around your own distracted or multitasking behaviors, here are a few questions to ask yourself each morning as you prepare for the day:

1. What is your intention for the day?

2. What are the most important outcomes you could achieve today, taking into account existing commitments (travel, meetings, conference calls, etc.)?

3. Do you need anything you don't already have (reference materials, supporting documents, etc.)? If so, arranging to get them may be your first task. It's a real killer to finally sit down to work on the budget, for example, and then have to scurry around trying to get your hands on the input you need from someone else.

4. Do you need to block time on your calendar for any particular task or project?

5. Do you need to arrange a different work space so you won't be interrupted?

6. Can you shut off your e-mail program for part of the day, or at least turn off the notification alerts?

7. Can you turn off or forward your phone?

Once you have thought through what you want to accomplish, equipped yourself with the reference materials or tools you will need, and allotted suitable time for the work, make certain you clear your work space of everything except for the task at hand and what you will need to work on it.

At the end of the day, review what you accomplished, give yourself a pat on the back, and notice if anything needs to carry over to the next day so you can start this list of questions all over tomorrow.

ﻵ

Conclusion: Workarounds Get Things Done

As you venture forward in your life, no doubt you will continue to chafe against roadblocks or obstacles of one kind or another that will require some kind of workaround on your part. The most powerful thing you can do when laid low with the frustrations that will surely arise is to keep your mind focused on your positive intention. Stay focused on what you want and why it matters. At the same time, you will also need to keep in mind that the other guy also wants something and that it probably matters to this person as well. Remember there are several core ingredients to successful workarounds, any one of which may be sufficient to get you through. There will also be times when you will need to blend several of these workaround ingredients to arrive at a recipe that will work for you. First and foremost:

THE MASTER SECRET: INTENTION VERSUS METHOD

If you allow yourself to lose sight of your purpose or intention, then you will be unlikely to find a successful workaround and will instead become preoccupied with the hurdle in front of you. Remember that old country saying: If you don't know where you are going, any road will do. Once you clarify your intention and commit to it, you may begin to discover multiple ways to get there. After that, make certain that you are fully committed to arriving at your desired outcome. As noted earlier, 99 percent won't get you there.

RESPONSE-ABILITY: CONTROL, INFLUENCE, RESPOND

Whenever you encounter a roadblock of any kind, remember to always look to yourself first for assistance. Ask what is within your own power to control, something you can do without needing to enlist anyone else in order to make a difference. No matter the situation or circumstance, you always will have some choices in the matter, the foremost of which is how you choose to respond, your response-ability.

If you need to get someone on board to get your workaround working, look first to anything you can handle on your own. By taking control of that which is truly yours, you will be in a much more powerful and influential position when you reach out to influence the choices someone else may need to make. If you have taken control of that which is yours and done what you can to influence others, you will then be in the best position to respond effectively to outside circumstances, even those that seem out of your control.

You will be wowed at how many situations you can impact by virtue of asking yourself that one unambiguous question: "What could I do that would make a difference that requires no one's permission other than my own?" I cannot emphasize this enough. People have so much more power over circumstances than they ever imagine. Keep your intention clear, do what you can on your own, and be prepared for unprecedented results.

PEOPLE DO THINGS FOR *THEIR* REASONS, NOT *YOUR* REASONS

We all know the advice about walking a mile in someone's shoes. Even if the other guy seems completely unreasonable or irrational, that's probably not how he or she sees the situation. Pause a few moments when you feel blocked by people to ask yourself why their choices might make sense to them. What might that underlying reason be? If you can come up with one or two possible explanations, first the others will lose some of the trappings of the adversarial role you might have assigned them, and then you may discover workaround options for greater influence. Often, by helping them to find a way to win, you will find ways of helping yourself.

Although it's not always the way it unfolds, following Larry Senn's advice to "assume innocence" will probably help more than it hinders. At a minimum, you will be pretty secure in assuming that the parties in question are making choices that they perceive will work best for them in the long run. Seeking to understand what motivates the other guy will always serve you well.

ACCOUNTABILITY: OWN THE GOAL, OWN THE PROCESS

If you are clear about your intentions, have made your responseable choices, and have taken others into consideration, the only thing left is to go for it 100 percent and embrace the results as yours. If things go bump in the night along the way, it will serve you much better in the long run if you ask yourself how you could have been better prepared so that these kinds of obstacles are avoided the next time. If you allow yourself to revert to complaining or blaming, you will drain off a considerable amount of your power to make choices and to influence others.

HOW YOU FRAME THE PROBLEM IS THE PROBLEM

Effective workaround strategies almost always come down to you: how are you framing the problem, what is your intention, and what choices do you have available to you? Are you complaining, or are you willing to risk going after what you prefer? As a dear friend is fond of saying, "When a pickpocket looks at an angel, all he sees are pockets." Now, I know that guidance may sound a bit strange, but I love it! I use it to keep me focused on what matters more than the obstacles in the way. If all I can see are the road-blocks, I might as well leave the car in the garage!

The more clarity you have on where you are headed, the more choices you will perceive. Keep in mind that your primary response-ability comes down to your willingness to control what you can, seek to influence from there, and then simply respond as best you can to everything else. People routinely lose sight of where they are headed, of what their true intentions are. Cut yourself some slack the next time you realize that you have lost track of your ultimate goal. We all do that.

As trite as it may seem, the secret to becoming successful at anything is to get up one more time than you fall down. If you think about it, you are probably pretty good at walking, and yet you have got up only one more time than you have fallen down. With practice, you have managed to put more and more time between falls. And, no matter how good you are at walking around, you will probably fall again. So, don't get caught in the blame game the next time you fall. Just notice, get up, and keep moving toward your desired outcome.

After all, if you don't move, you won't ever get there.

For more information about how Russell Bishop can help you with workarounds in your business, please visit us on the web at www .WorkaroundsThatWork.com or send an e-mail to Russell at Russell .Bishop@WorkaroundsThatWork.com.

Index